Song of Myself

The past and present wilt—I have fill'd them, emptied them.
And proceed to fill my next fold of the future.

Listener up there! what have you to confide to me?
Look in my face while I snuff the sidle of evening,
(Talk honestly, no one else hears you, and I stay only a minute longer.)

Do I contradict myself?
Very well then I contradict myself,
(I am large, I contain multitudes.)

I concentrate toward them that are nigh, I wait on the door-slab.

Who has done his day's work? who will soonest be through with his supper?
Who wishes to walk with me?

Will you speak before I am gone? will you prove already too late?

Walt Whitman, 1855

birthplace · state historic site · interpretive center

"I am large... I contain multitudes."

Featuring
Kwame Dawes
2023 WWBA Poet in Residence   **5.21.2023**

Copyright © 2024 Walt Whitman Birthplace
All rights reserved.

Published by Red Penguin Books

ISBN
Digital 978-1-63777-499-1
Print 978-1-63777-500-4

No part of this book may be reproduced in any form or by any electronic or mechanical means, including information storage and retrieval systems, without written permission from the author, except for the use of brief quotations in a book review.

All individual works are copyrighted to the writers.

Dear Readers,

The Walt Whitman Birthplace Association (WWBA) Board of Trustees and I congratulate the student poets in this anthology for their writing excellence! Each student internalized Whitman's poetic sentiments of *I am Large...I contain Multitudes* and created a unique response shaped in their own free verse poetry. We invite you to step into their world through the vision, words, and images of the 99 honorees of our *37th Annual 2023 Student Poetry Writing Contest*.

We received approximately 2200 entries from across the world, and a panel of published poets served as judges. We thank the judges for their professional collaboration. We acknowledge the students in this publication for their outstanding achievement, and we applaud their parents and teachers who guide and support their educational and creative endeavors.

Many new poets embrace poetic license. The Editors have aimed to remain true to the young poets' experimental use of free verse form as the students bravely struggle to embrace their multitudes. This collection celebrates their poetic voices and personal discoveries.

Kwame Dawes, the WWBA 2023 Poet in Residence, joined the celebration awards and offered words of praise and encouragement to the student poets. He read his poem, *Purple*, and contributed its printing and sale as a Limited-edition Broadside of 100 copies to support our education programs.

The Board and I deeply value our local, national, and international support which helps us to fulfill our mission to preserve and promote the legacy of Walt Whitman at this NY State Historic Site where he was born in 1819. Throughout the year, we host poetry readings and workshops, art exhibits, literary activities, community programs and seasonal family events. Do connect with us in person or virtually on our website: www.waltwhitman.org.

As a non-profit organization, the success of our programs is directly linked to the generosity of individuals like you who understand the importance of the unique role we serve. Please support our mission in any way that appeals to you – join, donate, sponsor, visit, volunteer, promote!

Let us now celebrate the young poets in this Anthology. The Trustees and I look forward to their continued literary accomplishments in the spirit of Walt Whitman.

Sincerely,

Cynthia Shor
WWBA Executive Director

Kwame Dawes

Emmy-winning Jamaican poet and writer Kwame Dawes, nicknamed "the Busiest Man in Literature" for his prolific library of published works, is the 2023 WWBA Poet in Residence. Dawes is a writer of poetry, fiction, nonfiction, and plays. He is the author of twenty books of poetry and numerous other volumes of fiction, criticism, and essays.

Born in Ghana in 1962, he moved to Jamaica in 1971 and spent most of his childhood and early adult life on the Caribbean Island. As a poet, he is profoundly influenced by the rhythms and textures of that lush place, citing in an interview his "spiritual, intellectual, and emotional engagement with reggae music."

Indeed, his book *Bob Marley: Lyrical Genius* remains the most authoritative study of the lyrics of Bob Marley.

Of his sixteen collections of poetry, his most recent titles include *Bivouac* (Akashic Books, 2019), *Duppy Conqueror* (Copper Canyon, 2013), shortlisted for the PEN Open Book Award, *Wheels* (2011), *Back of Mount Peace* (2009), *Hope's Hospice* (2009), *Impossible Flying* (2007), and *Gomer's Song* (2007). *Progeny of Air* (Peepal Tree, 1994) was a finalist for the Patterson Memorial Prize and was the winner of the Forward Poetry Prize for Best First Collection in the UK.

His most recent collection is *Nebraska* (UNP, 2019), a traverse into the intersection of memory, home, and artistic invention. He was also among the 2018 recipients of the Windham-Campbell Prize for Poetry.

Purple
Kwame Dawes

For Akua

Walking, I drew my hand over the lumpy
bloom of a spray of purple; I stripped away
my fingers, stained purple; put it to my nose,

the minty honey, a perfume so aggressively
pleasant—I gave it to you to smell,
my daughter, and you pulled away as if

I was giving you a palm full of wasps,
deceptions: "Smell the way the air
changes because of purple and green."

This is the promise I make to you:
I will never give you a fist full of wasps,
just the surprise of purple and the scent of rain.

*Reprinted by the Walt Whitman Birthplace Association
West Hills, Long Island, to commemorate Kwame Dawes's tenure as
43rd Poet in Residence for the year of 2023.*

Acknowledgments

Cynthia Shor, Executive Director, would like to thank the Board of Trustees who offer their outstanding guidance and support for all Association endeavors. Together, they extend the following acknowledgements on behalf of the Walt Whitman Birthplace Association (WWBA):

We thank all the student poets in this anthology who sustain the spirit of Walt Whitman with their creative and diverse voices. We thank all parents, teachers and mentors who foster poetry by teaching the value of words.

WWBA offers gratitude to our annual Poets in Residence, specifically Kwame Dawes this year, who serve to illuminate and fulfill the legacy of Walt Whitman with their teachings and own writing. We thank the contest judges, Nancy Keating, Matt Pasca and Christina Rau, poets themselves who read every poem and delight in celebrating the creative verses of the students.

We especially thank Lisa Pulitzer, Education Director, and Publisher Stephanie Larkin of Red Penguin Books, who worked tirelessly on the many drafts of this manuscript. We are also grateful to former Administrator Alyssa Abesamis and Graphic Designer Alana Abesamis who worked pro bono on the time-consuming first draft.

We thank the professional staff who make all our educational programs happen so effortlessly. Our programs are facilitated by Curator Margaret Guardi, Event & Media Director Heather Famiglietti, Administrator Derry Shafer, Controller Bonnie Meder, Poetry Writing Teachers Linda Trott Dickman and Laurie Rozakis, PhD, Art Educator Lena Sawyer, Docents Allison Bouton, Jim Broten, Jack Canfora, Lou Friedman, Iris Jumper, Jonathan Kalish, Danny Korez, Bryan Maccarrone, Barbara Nelson, Cameron Williams and Donna Varon, long term Volunteers Bruce Johnson, Lauren Montgomery, Nancy Newkirk and Alice Wilson, and a multitude of smart seasonal Interns. A special thanks to our loyal Whitman Personator Darrel Blaine Ford, who makes sure Whitman shows up every year for all the students.

WWBA offers appreciation to New York State Office of Parks, Recreation and Historic Preservation with individual recognition going to Governor Kathy Hochul, Parks Commissioner Eric Kulleseid, and Long Island Regional Director George Gorman. We greatly thank Suffolk County for their outstanding and generous support, and we acknowledge The Town of Huntington who nurtured Walt during his formative years and who continues to nurture his legacy today. We extend our appreciation to grantors Humanities New York, NYS Council on the Arts, Huntington Arts Council, The Claire Friedlander Family Foundation, and Poets & Writers for their support of literature, literacy, and learners.

We acknowledge with great appreciation our members, donors and sponsors whose contributions sustain the daily operations of the Walt Whitman Birthplace State Historic Site, and whose actions sustain the spirit of Walt Whitman.

Contents

CATEGORY A INDIVIDUAL POEM, GRADES 3 & 4

Emily's Poem — 2
Emily Gravitz, LAKEVILLE
ELEMENTARY SCHOOL
GRAND CHAMPION

The poem of me — 3
Julian Carazo, MILLS POND
ELEMENTARY SCHOOL

Tumbled — 4
John Connors, MOUNT SINAI
ELEMENTARY SCHOOL

All About Me — 5
Valerie Kong, A. P. WILLITS
ELEMENTARY SCHOOL

Song of myself — 6
Nolan Maliszewski, MILLS POND
ELEMENTARY SCHOOL

All About Me — 7
Michael Marchello, JUDY JACOBS-
PARKWAY ELEMENTARY SCHOOL

I'm Me — 8
Amisha Pahar, BURNS AVENUE
ELEMENTARY SCHOOL

This is Me, A Beautiful Me   9
Radhika Prajapati, BURNS AVENUE
ELEMENTARY SCHOOL

A Song of my Contradictions   10
Maggie Rubin, NORTH SIDE
ELEMENTARY SCHOOL

Dreams of A Journey   11
Aria Russell, SOUTHAMPTON
ELEMENTARY SCHOOL

Me!   12
Ava Sprague, MOUNT SINAI
ELEMENTARY SCHOOL

My Habits for Life   13
Calissa Wong, ELIZABETH M. BAKER
ELEMENTARY SCHOOL

CATEGORY B   INDIVIDUAL POEM, GRADES 5 & 6

I was Born with Autumn's Leaves 16
Alexeen Dillon, THE LAUREL HILL
SCHOOL
GRAND CHAMPION

Your Mom   17
Samia Ahmed, BAY SHORE MIDDLE
SCHOOL

Flaws and Awes   18
Zainab Chowdhury, W.T. CLARKE
MIDDLE SCHOOL

Essence of My Being   19
Ford Duchatelier Beaubrun, BAY SHORE
MIDDLE SCHOOL

Containing Multitudes   20
Daniel Garcia, THE LAUREL HILL
SCHOOL

A DAD I NEVER KNEW   21
Ava Grello, BAY SHORE MIDDLE SCHOOL

Cracked and Crumbled   22
Yael Mozes, THE LAUREL HILL SCHOOL

Who I Am   23
Zaynab Najimi, SUNQUAM ELEMENTARY SCHOOL

You and I   24
Riley Wagner, EDWARD J. BCSTI ELEMENTARY SCHOOL

Friends and Me   25
Lauren Wells, JOHN F. KENNEDY ELEMENTARY SCHOOL

Inside The Nutshell   26
Elizabeth Wilkinson, THE LAUREL HILL SCHOOL

CATEGORY C   INDIVIDUAL POEM, GRADES 7 & 8

Untitled   30
Rebecca Henneman, SAINT ANN'S SCHOOL
GRAND CHAMPION

Anywhere   31
Ally Angell, W.T. CLARKE MIDDLE SCHOOL

Crochet   32
Kiana Bonifacio, TUCKAHOE COMMON MIDDLE SCHOOL

Endless Flow   33
Amartya Das, R.C. MURPHY JUNIOR HIGH SCHOOL

Evolving   34
Emmanuel Halkias, MANHASSET MIDDLE SCHOOL

My Knot of Life   35
Allie E. Harrison, P.J. GELINAS JUNIOR HIGH SCHOOL

Fraud   36
Andalucia Navetta, WANTAGH MIDDLE SCHOOL

Puzzle   37
Anna Regan, CARRIE P. WEBER MIDDLE SCHOOL

Healing a Tree   38
Isabelle Rubino, MOUNT SINAI MIDDLE SCHOOL

My Name   39
Koharu Sato, MANHASSET MIDDLE SCHOOL

Unaware   40
Jacob Torczyner, HEBREW ACADEMY OF LONG BEACH

Reflection   41
Valerie Torres, SPRINGS SCHOOL

The Multitudes   42
Oliver Won, GREAT NECK SOUTH MIDDLE SCHOOL

BIRD AND ME   43
Nancy Yu, NEW HYDE PARK MEMORIAL HIGH SCHOOL

CATEGORY D INDIVIDUAL POEM, GRADES 9 & 10

I Am   46
Ava Kuklis, WESTHAMPTON BEACH
HIGH SCHOOL
GRAND CHAMPION

house of cards   48
Rina Olsen, SAINT JOHN'S SCHCOL
GRAND CHAMPION

A mosaic   50
Anika Amin, SAINT ANN'S SCHOOL

Paper Cranes   51
Hannah Bahn, SAINT ANN'S SCHOOL

Me, Moment   52
Sophia Bergeron, SOUTH LYON EAST
HIGH SCHOOL

Sister   53
Colleen Carroll, EASTPORT-SOUTH
MANOR JUNIOR-SENIOR HIGH
SCHOOL

Unabated Passion…   54
Multitudes 2023
AnnaBelle Deaner, HALF HOLLOW
HILLS HIGH SCHOOL EAST

Ink, Coffee & Postage Stamps   56
Giuliana DePaola, FLORAL PARK
MEMORIAL HIGH SCHOOL

To Know You, Is to Know Me   57
Isabella Fernandim, SACRED HEART
ACADEMY

Home   58
Anelisa Fulgieri, WELLINGTON C.
MEPHAM HIGH SCHOOL

American   59
Emilin George, NEW HYDE PARK MEMORIAL HIGH SCHOOL

The Beauty of the World   60
Isabella Gonzalez, LONG BEACH HIGH SCHOOL

Girl of Sand   61
Cate Grady, SACRED HEART ACADEMY

Even Blue Has Multitudes   62
Rachel Ha, HERRICKS HIGH SCHOOL

Jew(ish)   63
Isabella Kohl, ROSLYN HIGH SCHOOL

Spear of Summer Grass   64
Caitlin Lee, HERRICKS HIGH SCHOOL

All and More   65
Julia Milos, OYSTER BAY HIGH SCHOOL

Jazve   66
Vladamir Mkrtchian, WELLINGTON C. MEPHAM HIGH SCHOOL

Memories of Mine   67
Ariana Muhammad, NEW HYDE PARK MEMORIAL HIGH SCHOOL

Bulletproof Legacy   68
Rizwan Rumi, NEW HYDE PARK MEMORIAL HIGH SCHOOL

Goldfish   69
Natalia Sanchez, SMITHTOWN HIGH SCHOOL WEST

Unheard Melody   70
Ashna Shah, SYOSSET HIGH SCHOOL

A Long Way to Go   71
Siddhanth R. Surya, NEW HYDE PARK MEMORIAL HIGH SCHOOL

If I Were Free   72
Jaclyn Xue, PLAINVIEW-OLD BETHPAGE JOHN F. KENNEDY HIGH SCHOOL

CATEGORY E   INDIVIDUAL POEM, GRADES 11 & 12

Traveling Pots   76
Hannah Ninan, NEW HYDE PARK MEMORIAL HIGH SCHOOL
GRAND CHAMPION

sixth period   77
Rainer Pasca, BAY SHORE HIGH SCHOOL
GRAND CHAMPION

Burn Scars   78
Lyla Forest Butler, SAINT ANN'S SCHOOL

This Is All You Need To Know   79
Lyla Forest Butler, SAINT ANN'S SCHOOL

Happiness   80
Luis Corvera, UNIONDALE HIGH SCHOOL

Terrible, just Awful (People, not the poem itself)   81
Seth Del Orbe, NEW HYDE PARK MEMORIAL HIGH SCHOOL

The Vine that Swallowed the South   82
Adelrhany Georges, WALT WHITMAN HIGH SCHOOL

places visited 83
Queenie Liu, NEW HYDE PARK
MEMORIAL HIGH SCHOOL

Burdens 84
Adelyn Loh, HERRICKS HIGH SCHOOL

The War of Individuality 85
Paige MacPherson, WALT WHITMAN
HIGH SCHOOL

Fluid 86
Candida Villalta Meza, WALT WHITMAN
HIGH SCHOOL

Sky Lanterns 87
Allison Xu, WALTER JOHNSON HIGH
SCHOOL

Multitudes 88
Emily Grace Zabala, NEW HYDE PARK
MEMORIAL HIGH SCHOOL

CATEGORY F — INDIVIDUAL ANTHOLOGY

Whispers Across the Fields 93
Christina Pan, PLAINVIEW-OLD
BETHPAGE JOHN F. KENNEDY HIGH
SCHOOL
GRAND CHAMPION

CATEGORY G — CLASS ANTHOLOGY, GRADES 3 & 4

Glitter Upon Mountains 97
Ms. Zucaro 3rd Grade Class, FORT
SALONGA ELEMENTARY SCHOOL
GRAND CHAMPION

CATEGORY I   CLASS ANTHOLOGY, GRADES 7 & 8

About Us   100
Ms. Pomaro 8th Grade Period 2 Class,
MOUNT SINAI MIDDLE SCHOOL
GRAND CHAMPION

A Multitude of Poems   101
(Volume 1)
Mrs. Wallace 7th Grade Period 1 Class,
MOUNT SINAI MIDDLE SCHOOL

A Multitude of Poems   101
(Volume 2)
Mrs. Wallace 8th Grade Period 2 Class,
MOUNT SINAI MIDDLE SCHOOL

A Multitude of Poems   101
(Volume 3)
Mrs. Wallace 8th Grade Period 3 Class,
MOUNT SINAI MIDDLE SCHOOL

A Multitude of Poems   102
(Volume 4)
Mrs. Wallace 8th Grade Period 3 Class,
MOUNT SINAI MIDDLE SCHOOL

A Multitude of Poems   102
(Volume 5)
Mrs. Wallace 8th Grade Period 9 Class,
MOUNT SINAI MIDDLE SCHOOL

Chapters of Life   102
Ms. Doran 7th Grade Period 3 Class,
MOUNT SINAI MIDDLE SCHOOL

Everyone's Story   103
Ms. Doran 7th Grade Period 8 Class,
MOUNT SINAI MIDDLE SCHOOL

Listen to Who I Am   103
Ms. Doran 7th Grade Period 7 Class,
MOUNT SINAI MIDDLE SCHOOL

The Many Parts That   103
Make Us Whole
Ms. Pomaro 8th Grade Period 9 Class,
Mount Sinai Middle School

CATEGORY J   CLASS ANTHOLOGY, GRADES 9 & 10

Multitudes of Us   106
Ms. Murphy 9th Grade Period 3 Class,
OYSTER BAY HIGH SCHOOL
GRAND CHAMPION

Beauty and Grass   107
in All Things
Ms. Junjulas Grades 9–10,
MASSAPEQUA HIGH SCHOOL

We Are Multitudes   107
Ms. Martin 10th Grade Period 6 Class,
EASTPORT-SOUTH MANOR JUNIOR-
SENIOR HIGH SCHOOL

CATEGORY K   CLASS ANTHOLOGY, GRADES 11 & 12

Letters Unsent   110
Dr. Faughey 11th Grade Period 2 Class,
OYSTER BAY HIGH SCHOOL
GRAND CHAMPION

A Melodic Escape   111
Dr. Faughey 11th Grade Period 4 Class,
OYSTER BAY HIGH SCHOOL

All Shapes and Sizes   111
Ms. Martin 11th Grade Period 5 Class,
EASTPORT-SOUTH MANOR JUNIOR-
SENIOR HIGH SCHOOL

I Encompass Worlds   111
Ms. Cho 11th Grade Period 2 Class,
PLAINVIEW-OLD BETHPAGE JOHN F.
KENNEDY HIGH SCHOOL

Versions of Myself 112
Ms. Cho 11th Grade Period 4 Class,
PLAINVIEW-OLD BETHPAGE JOHN F.
KENNEDY HIGH SCHOOL

CATEGORY L MULTIMEDIA

My Hair That Makes Up Me 116
Malia Lockhart, MOUNT SINAI MIDDLE SCHOOL
GRAND CHAMPION

There is Time 118
Paige Sweeney, OYSTER BAY HIGH SCHOOL
GRAND CHAMPION

Only Me 120
Lily Dejesus, MOUNT SINAI MIDDLE SCHOOL

The Pursuit 122
Maiya Staudt, MOUNT SINAI MIDDLE SCHOOL

INDIVIDUAL POEM, GRADES 3 & 4

Category A

Emily's Poem
Emily Gravitz

you are connected to everything
you are every blade of grass
like every wildflower
you are different from all others
coral, sage, beige, even cobalt blue!
each unique and magnificent
like a kaleidoscope, every individual vibrant shape
takes form to create a masterpiece
like my mother, I am fluent in Chinese
my father's eyes can be seen in my smile
yet, I am not like the others
the talents I possess are uniquely my own
while others fail to draw a flower, I sketch it with ease
while others grumble and complain,
I solve math equations and read contentedly
yet I am not good at everything
while others do sports with ease,
I struggle with the simplest drill.
while others strive to be perfect,
I have learned that perfection does not exist
we are the branches of our community
as different the branches are
and as far apart the branches may be
we are all part of the same tree

LAKEVILLE ELEMENTARY SCHOOL
Ms. Pellegrini, Grade 4

The poem of me
Julian Carazo

I am good at art
Only cartoons
Sometimes I sketch too
I know about history
Of the good and the bad
The color I like is black
I come from the country of the Archangel Miguel
And the diablo that is Lucifer
And the Virgin of the Socavon
I want to go to the country of Fidel and Che
I may be from the country of Tango
And I have Quechua blood of the Andes
I am interested in 1980's marketing
My taste in music is Barry Manilow
Not just a singer
But a performer
My favorite food is pique macho
Made from the Andes
I also come from the country of soccer and Cartagena
I am interested in the violent sport of boxing
And I am good at soccer
The countries I come from are filled with culture
From Archangel Miguel to tango to salsa.

Tumbled
John Connors

I swim in the water,
A fish in the sea,
Duck under the waves,
Dive through the watery doorway.
I have to be virtuous.
When a big wave comes and washes me in,
The sand scrapes my back,
Like tumbling in a washing machine.
Like a whale I make noise,
Yet no one can hear.
I don't know what to do.
Which way is up?
Which way is down?
Interminable disputes with no confutations,
Issue through my mind as a fast-narrow river.
I try to come up for a breath,
Pounded again,
I finally emerge,
I run to the sand.
Just like the waves,
Just like the sea,
I get pulled under,
Until I come up again!

Category A, Individual Poem Grades 3–4
MOUNT SINAI ELEMENTARY SCHOOL
Mr. Walsh, Grade 4

All About Me
Valerie Kong

I am smart.
I know the answer to every question.
If I don't, I will work hard to find one.
I am funny.
I make all my friends laugh with silly voices and actions.
You know that my baby sister thinks I'm funny too?
I am brave.
I stand up to bullies.
They don't make me whimper.
I play the piano and violin.
My fingers dance across the keys like swans gliding on the lake.
The bow swishes across the strings like an ice skater speeding on ice.
I love the winter, a fabulous wonder.
The snow sparkles like sequins on fabric.
As I make my silly snowman, I slip and slide on the ice - Whee! Whoosh!
I focus on things I do - reading, especially.
Reading shuttles me to a different place and different time.
I meet people from the past and in the future.
Diving into the stories, I visualize myself as the main character,
Facing challenges and growing mature through each adventure.
Reading is what I need to go on an exciting vacation or a lifelong journey.
I like the world I live in.
This world is full of wonders, though sometimes there is war, diseases and disasters.
During hard times, we unite.
We help each other; we encourage each other; we become stronger, and
We create a vigorous future together.
I enjoy my life and I am Me.
Multitudes help me be unique.
There are multitudes contained within me.

A. P. WILLITS ELEMENTARY SCHOOL
Mrs. McCloskey, Grade 4

Song of myself
Nolan Maliszewski

his mind is exploding with armies of ideas
he loves many things,
he loves chilling capybaras,
he loves savory starfruit,
he loves strenuous sports,
he loves the outrageous outdoors,
he loves his forever family,
he loves his colossal culture,

he experienced many things,
he experienced going to free-spirited Fire Island and seeing a spine-chilling shark,
he experienced going to mellow Montauk and getting crushed by the whopping waves,
he experienced going to fiery Florida watching a sailing stingray swim under his boogie board and seeing an idle iguana in a towering tree,
he experienced going to dazzling Disney and cheering on every ride in majestic Magic Kingdom,
he experienced rock climbing 12 feet up with no rope,
I am he

Category A, Individual Poem Grades 3–4
MILLS POND ELEMENTARY SCHOOL
Ms. Lopez, Grade 4

All About Me
Michael Marchello

My name is Michael,
and I have lots of hobbies you see.
I play basketball and math because those things are fun for me.
I have been to Florida, a beautiful place with big tall trees.
I go there with my family,
My mom, my dad and me!
My siblings trail along as well,
and when they get in trouble, my parents never yell!
I like to get a lot of sleep, I find it very great!
My brother sleeps later than me but we can still relate.
In the cellar him and me, spend our hours playing games.
Then outside in our backyard, our yard is like the planes!

JUDY JACOBS-PARKWAY ELEMENTARY SCHOOL
Ms. Korwan, Grade 4

I'm Me
Amisha Pahar

I Am me
Because I am smart like a heart.
I love cats who are in hats.
I love the sunlight but I get scared in the midnight
I love singing in my room
but when people hear me it is my doom!
My friends are the best just like the rest!
I love sleeping but hate weeping
I HATE bats but love cats
I love blue and love Gru too!
I love California. It's a blast. I hope my trip was not my last!
I love Christmas and school is my business
I love flowers but wish I had powers
When I read books I get hooked
I love my bed but HATE red
I love K-pop because they never flop
I hate math but love baths
I love ice cream in bowls but it feels better in cones
I love to doodle just how I love noodles
I love dreams but when it's too scary I SCREAM
I love the summer but I'm not a runner
I love me because I'm me
I love candy because it gets in handy
I'm the best because I'm not like the rest,
I am me, beautiful me

Category A, Individual Poem Grades 3–4
BURNS AVENUE ELEMENTARY SCHOOL
Ms. Urkiel, Grade 3

This is Me, A Beautiful Me
Radhika Prajapati

This is me, a beautiful me.
I am bright like the sun, but dark like the night.
I rise up like balloons and fall down like spiders.
I am kind like blossoms, but
I can be mean like a monster.
I am calm as the ocean and cool as the breeze.
I am big like a lion and small like a bee.
I bloom up like a flower and light up like a lantern.
I love the art of music that lies in me.
It's very powerful and joyful to me.
I like the winter cause you stay home and I love summer since you do the same thing.
You are you, and I am me.
We both have different possibilities.
I like rain, you like snow.
I like parts of the world I come across.
We both have different likings we see from each other.
This is me, a beautiful me.

Category A, Individual Poem Grades 3–4
BURNS AVENUE ELEMENTARY SCHOOL
Ms. Urkiel, Grade 4

A Song of my Contradictions
Maggie Rubin

Do I contradict myself? Very well then, I contradict myself.
I love gymnastics for bars and vault
But I don't like it for beam and floor
I contradict myself.
I am scared of trying new foods
But I am brave on rollercoasters
I contradict myself.
I am calm and sweet during yoga
But I am aggressive and competitive during roughhousing
I contradict myself.
Yes, it is true. So, this is what I have to say:
The world is filled with joy and love
But sometimes we feel sadness and dislike
and that is just fine.
We are large. We contain multitudes.
Myself is Maggie, and that's just fine too.

Category A, Individual Poem Grades 3–4
NORTH SIDE ELEMENTARY SCHOOL
Ms. Trustey, Grade 3

Dreams of A Journey
Aria Russell

Dream big. Dream tall.
Be proud. Don't fall.

Work hard. Be kind.
Don't lie, in your right mind.

Just try to be good.
Be super, like your hero would.

You are you.
And I am me.

Let us fill each other with glee.

You choose them.
I choose you.

We are different.
But friends too!

Me!
Ava Sprague

I'm not like you,
but yet I am.
We are all unique,
And complicated.

Things terrify us,
We are startled for reasons of our own.
I'm completely horrified of DEATH!
It means my journey is over.

Many things also make us uneasy,
I get sorrowful when I get bad grades,
I adore many things too,
I'm very loving of my dog, Axel,

Great reflexes like a panther,
Fast as a cheetah,
Smart as an octopus,
And as fierce as a tiger,
Animals remind me of myself.

And at night,
I lay down,
Concentrate and think,
Ponder about what I've done,
And brood about the future,
What will it offer me?
Will I have the same dream?
The dream to become a soccer player?
I doze off knowing,
That I am large,
I contain multitudes.

MOUNT SINAI ELEMENTARY SCHOOL
Mr. Walsh, Grade 4

My Habits for Life
Calissa Wong

My school teaches us habits for life,
They help us understand one another
By being respectful, loving, and caring.
We always need to be kind, try our best and persevere,
Be generous, helpful, compassionate and empathetic to others.

Even though I have trouble expressing myself through writing,
My teacher, family and classmates are supportive and encourage me.
When I play soccer and I miss a goal,
My teammates and coach reassure me and I learn from my mistake.
Be thankful, always forgive and be inclusive to others.

These are my habits for life.
Why don't you give it a try?
I know that these will help you grow.
Just remember to be considerate, honest and truthful to yourself and others
By welcoming everyone and be a bucket-filler!

ELIZABETH M. BAKER ELEMENTARY SCHOOL
Mrs. Greenspoon, Grade 3

INDIVIDUAL POEM, GRADES 5 & 6

Category B

Grand Champion

I was Born with Autumn's Leaves
Alexeen Dillon

I was born with autumn's leaves
Ever changing like me.

In a way I give air
You will just never see.

Rain pours down with just one hope,
To feed spring's plants and watch them grow.
Yet, you are there providing air for all,
Like me, small things make a difference for all.

As the sun comes up on a hot summer day
It tells kids it is time to play.
But you are exhausted, tired, and deflated.
Like me you push on
For we know we are providing
Something strong.

When winter comes, it says be gone
It puts you down, you are swallowed in its frost
Little do you know, you are being used
Only to do something for the greater good.

The leaves in the seasons
They are ever changing like me
They are there unnoticed, doing something amazing.

We are the colors of life
We are part of a great cycle
We are made up of many multitudes.

I was born with autumn's leaves.

Category B, Individual Poem Grades 5–6
THE LAUREL HILL SCHOOL
Mrs. Bird, Grade 6

Your Mom
Samia Ahmed

(poem is very exaggerated)

I am large...
I contain many multitudes
I am a meadow of traits quite vast
But, like in any field,
There are always some patches of dead grass
This field of mine stretches far and wide
The most productive and plentiful meadows in LI
In New Jersey, the most vibrant and full of family
Lush and sunny, never a worry about money
And in Amman, the driest of land
Sun–baked and dehydrated, nothing but miles of sand
My side of the meadow, though barren and strained
Is fed well by Long Island's never-ending rain
Some days
Or every day,
The rain pounds a little too hard
Shattering my brain into a million little shards
Suddenly the blade in my drawer starts to glint
Almost as though giving me a hint
But I force myself to turn away
Cutting your skin will only make you decay
Instead, I take some time to think
And soon enough, I find myself at the ice rink
Using a different kind of blade, I slice ice
Carving letters with my skate, each line precise
Spiraling, gliding, and occasionally sliding
It doesn't feel cold, just warmly inviting
My skates do the work, my legs stay relaxed
The blades know where to go, even without tracks
On rainy days like these, skating is my form of therapy.

the end.

Flaws and Awes
Zainab Chowdhury

I am like a camera capturing my flaws and awes,
One moment you see red another yellow,
My anger comes and goes,
Some days I am high others I am low,
Just like the pitch of my saxophone,

While those are some flaws,
I have much more awes,

I am like seasons,
Joyful and bright like summer,
Shy like winter,
Beautiful like spring,
Artistic like fall,

I can be a pineapple,
Standing tall with a crown,
Having a sweet taste on the inside,

Sometimes I think I am nothing,
But I know I am something,
I can be anything,
But nothing can be me.

Category B, Individual Poem Grades 5–6
W.T. CLARKE MIDDLE SCHOOL
Ms. Hartman, Grade 6

Essence of My Being
Ford Duchatelier-Beaubrun

A universe of multitudes resides in my soul
A heart full of empathy and compassion
And a head chock full of goals
An innovator, writer, speaker, humanitarian and good student are some of my roles
Within me, are a plethora of contradictions filled to the brim
My light is bright, it is not dim
I am the quiet of the dawn and the roar of the ocean at morn
The solitude of the mountain peak, and the busyness of a city street
I am the music of the spheres, and the thumping beat of a heart that loves and fears
The words of a poem that speaks, and the colors of a canvas that leaks
Beautiful art that speaks to the mind, seek and you will find that books nourish my imagination
My brain is the intense acceleration of a sports car, and the drear of a thunderstorm
A collage of scattered yet together thoughts and ideas, and the order of a form
A myriad of idiosyncrasies, peculiarities and eccentricities make up myself
My passion for science, and my interest in health
Aspirations of delivering speeches in front of the entire nation, and leading a country
Environmental activism, and planting an Oak tree
Dreams of becoming a neuroscientist and studying the cerebrum
Being in a band and playing the snare drum
Quirks, qualities, and everything in between
I am nature's beauty to be seen
The places I have been, and the places I will go
A world of adventure to explore and know
So within me, multitudes thrive
A reflection of the way I strive
A journey that is never fully done
In my blood are my ancestors, who walked so I can run

BAY SHORE MIDDLE SCHOOL
Mr. Curtis, Grade 6

Containing Multitudes
Daniel Garcia

I am a river
I am fresh and I can be calm or harsh
I can be straightforward or complicated
I am easy going and gentle
I am a mountain
I have a peak and I soar up
I can be broken down
I can stand tall and be proud
I am a volcano
I burst with excitement and can control myself sometimes
I have a bright inside
I can burn all of the negativity inside
I am a tree
I start small and I can grow big
I have many elements inside
I can almost never die
I am a bird
I can reach new heights and I can have courage to fly
I take care of the little
I help the big
I am a book
I can make people laugh, cry, and wonder
I can have information
I never leave people hanging
I am myself
I care for others and I am funny
I have the power to love
I stand out when others do not
And I am myself

Category B, Individual Poem Grades 5–6
THE LAUREL HILL SCHOOL
Mrs. Bird, Grade 5

A DAD I NEVER KNEW
Ava Grello

A dad I never knew
But still I pretend
That I knew his voice, face, and friends
When my mom gets unhappy and downhearted
Because of that fateful day
I can never relate to that space left unguarded
All those sorry's and words filled with pity
Make me feel worse
Did he like dogs?
I don't know
Did he?
Alas, I was shaped by others
Molded from a lump of clay
Rockin' to Bon Jovi at 10 pm
Singing in the shower to some song that's SO cliche
My mother showed me manners and consequence
My sister showed friendship, humor and strength
My head boppin' playlist
The jokes I come to tell
The things I laugh about
And the person I've become now
From my friends it was experiences
Good times always cherished
Laughing so hard, till the point that I'm crying
I try to be kind, but really I'm greedy
Always wanting my sister to come home more
To go upstate and visit friends very missed
But all these people poured love in my heart and stood by me all the way
Shaped me into the person I've become and still becoming today

Cracked and Crumbled
Yael Mozes

High achiever is what they see
They never read between the lines
Raised on reality
To be the very best
To take all advice
To live with an injured heart
When their words mess with my head
They all come back again
Saying they did not realize
How to use their weapons
And I'm suddenly drowning
Surrounded by darkness
And the ones that never cared
I have myself
And I have the privilege to love it
Darkness now drained
In my ocean of tears
With my hair in my face
And the bruises that scar it
I know I cannot escape them
I cannot hide from them
I learn that my flaws are the criminals behind my pain
I think about this and I rephrase
I learn that my flaws are the criminals behind my pain
And they are beautiful.

Who I Am
Zaynab Najimi

On days when I am sad...
I am a cold flower in the winter
But those days rarely come
On days when I feel joyous...
I am the Sun shining down brightly
And those days are my most common

I am not the one who will follow
I am the one who will lead
The multitudes inside me continue to grow
As my feelings change, so do I
The emotions inside me spread
Until I feel they are going to burst
My feelings will change in time
My anger will turn to laughter
My joy will turn to despair
But that's just life
There's no stopping that
Although I am different from the rest,
I know that I will shine brighter than them all

But the deepest layers of me
Are the ones that no one knows
I didn't know them either
But I soon started to look in deep
And then...
I found who I am

SUNQUAM ELEMENTARY SCHOOL
Ms. Monroe, Grade 5

You and I
Riley Wagner

I see someone who is alike,
Yet different from me.

I see the light sun,
But you see the dark moon.

I see tall,
But you see short.

I get 8 painful teeth pulled,
But you have all perfect 28!

You take the long route
But I am trying to get out of there right away.

I like the juicy steak,
But you like the mushy side.

I like the old country side,
But you like the big city.

I dribble the ball up the field
But you are standing still as a goalpost.

I dream it,
But you believe it!

I see someone who is alike,
Yet different from me.

Category B, Individual Poem Grades 5–6
EDWARD J. BOSTI ELEMENTARY SCHOOL
Mrs. Zalewski, Grade 5

Friends and Me
Lauren Wells

I stand there as one person
Watching more and more
People by the scent I have
Blonde hair you have black
I hear you singing you watch
Me do nothing standing in
The back you say why so
Sad I say just lonely you
Say why not come sing with
Me I say sure we sing and sing
Like 2 chirping birds until we finally
Go back to the nest.

Inside The Nutshell
Elizabeth Wilkinson

Inside the nutshell are many things to seek,
Many things there are, music and sports galore.
Drawings in halls,
And no, my family's not small,
Yes, there are other people indeed.

Do I like to draw, to be up in my room?
Well, yes, very much,
But also, I like to run around and play,

I enjoy playing guitar and hanging out at parties.
Do I contradict myself?
Yes, but in a very good way.

Like I said, there are many people too,
Many people that make me, who?
Inside the nutshell, there are many things to see.
Inside the nutshell are the things...
The things that make me... me

Category B, Individual Poem Grades 5–6
THE LAUREL HILL SCHOOL
Mrs. Bird, Grade 6

INDIVIDUAL POEM, GRADES 7 & 8

Category C

Grand Champion

Untitled
Rebecca Henneman

There is no silence anymore
sinking into the deep blue
swimming in your gaze
I do not see them anymore
pulling my arms into your lap
rubbing over my soft skin with your coarse hands
whispering praise
I am trained to long for your voice
laying out on the splintered wood floor
floating in pools of sunlight
dripping onto my body
I don't need you to say you're sorry
nevermind your sullen looks
that ripples fear throughout my skeleton
shaking and shivering because your face says the end
don't make me leave so soon
return to the soft smiles that melt my heart
into a bloody sea
don't throw knives instead
stabbing gashes that rip through the muscle
return to me
return to us

Category C, Individual Poem Grades 7–8
SAINT ANN'S SCHOOL
Ms. Mascarenhas, Grade 8

Anywhere
Ally Angell

When the world crumbles to ashes,
cold and dull and gray,
I'd like to travel anywhere,
to chase the fog away.

A heavenly white castle,
pristine and draped with lace,
engulfed in balmy, golden hour,
clouds with pearls in place.

A shimmering dark oak tree,
wood's air hazy, thick,
all hollowed out, spilling with warmth,
the brook, gold fireflies prick.

A fragrant field of wildflowers,
sky a pure blue slate,
tulips rainbow, grass bright green,
A golden sunlit gate.

When dreary worlds are black and white,
all mixed to the same hue,
like age-old paint discarded,
left to look for something new,

I turn to my vast vibrant mind,
dimensions bright with glory,
for when I travel anywhere,
It's I who write my story!

Crochet
Kiana Bonifacio

Touch—my fingers slip around the smooth pallet
Smell—the citrus-like aroma drifting through the air
See-

My fingers drift across the yarn.
It's as scratchy as cotton.
Blue, yellow, purple, which one.
I pick up my crocheting hook, the familiarity welcomes me
The feel of my hook is like home to me

A slipknot here
A whipstitch there

One, two, three, four
Cannot lose count
Five, six, seven, eight

Chain after chain
Stitch by stitch
Row after row

Red blisters throbbing on my fingers that pull tight
I work well into the night
But only when I have light by my side

My hands walk the rows of yarn
Turning, bending, to a yarned music

Thousands of colors tangle at once before my eyes
warm, cozy gifts, it's your surprise

Ask me nicely and I may agree
If I can make something gorgeous for you
With hook and yarn as I'm known to do

Category C, Individual Poem Grades 7–8
TUCKAHOE COMMON MIDDLE SCHOOL
Ms. Goldberg, Grade 7

Endless Flow
Amartya Das

I am an endless flow
Like a burbling brook flowing through a forest
With dappled afternoon sunlight illuminating me
And like a placid lake
The calm moon shining brilliantly on my surface
And like the mighty ocean
My waves tearing through the deep gloom of night

I am an endless flow
When the scorching sun beams upon me
I wither away, ascending toward the heavens
Yet as time passes in the dark
I recollect myself, solidifying once again
And fall, raging, pounding the world below
As I return to momentary peace

I am an endless flow
Waning and ebbing tirelessly
Every light reflects off my crystal-like surface differently
Completely changing my appearance
Burbling, roaring, or gently swaying
What is my true form?
No one can ever truly know

I am an endless flow

Evolving
Emmanuel Halkias

They came before me
Generations
Boys bearing the burdens of men
Suffering unspeakable losses
They had no desks, no lessons
Schooled only by fear, injustice, and life's experiences
Laying foundations with their dreams
They became legends
Defined by their grit and pride and the expectations they left behind
Evolving every day
I climb onto their broad shoulders
The time has come for me to leave my mark
Looking forward and looking back
I tremble with inevitable fear because my future remains unclear
I am standing at the precipice
Do I fall
Or do I soar?

MANHASSET MIDDLE SCHOOL
Mrs. Pellegrino, Grade 8

My Knot of Life
Allie E. Harrison

Life's an intricate paradox,
A complicated knot,
With many threads and twists and loops,
Some clear, and some are not.

I am one who appreciates
Spending time alone.
However, I have many friends
I love down to the bone.

I, myself, am surely not
The aggressive, hostile sort.
Nonetheless, fencing is
My very favorite sport.

Despite all this, some parts of me
Do go hand in hand.
Reading and writing are two passions
That burn within me like a brand.

Some threads of my own life may seem
To clash, even collide.
But take one away and it'll all unravel—
My very life untied.

Life's an intricate paradox,
A complicated knot.
Some things make sense, and some things don't,
But cherish all you've got.

Category C, Individual Poem Grades 7–8
P.J. GELINAS JUNIOR HIGH SCHOOL
Ms. Palmer, Grade 8

Fraud
Andalucia Navetta

I stare at an impersonator.
The person looks like me
but doesn't feel like me.

I touch the person's hand
They touch mine too.
In sync yet
I pull away.

I reach for the corner of my face
The fraud does the same
I feel the corner of my skin
bending over
like a young child's
favorite paperback story.
I impulsively pull- it doesn't hurt.
The fake is holding an identical mask.

New layers peel, rinse and repeat.

The masks pile on the wooden floor like paper shreds
Behind the pretender, an identical pile.
I close my eyes and pull sharply
Mask after mask
Tears build up
Not because it hurts.

Relief.

Urged to pull again,
but the skin won't budge.
The bags under my eyes have sunken farther into my head
teeth yellowed, lips chapped.
Then I look up at the trickster
Then I see myself.

Am I a fraud?

WANTAGH MIDDLE SCHOOL
Mrs. Hult, Grade 8

Puzzle
Anna Regan

The surface is assembled like a perfect brick wall
But over time bits of pieces start to fall and crack but it still stands up high
Time is what causes tiny holes in perfection, but it will never fall
Putting an eye to the hole to see what's beyond.

Hypnotized by the chaos and confused by what's seen
My mind is complex to those who don't know me
I can see things no one else can see
The cracks on the surface, the wall starting to lean.

I am a 5000 piece puzzle with just one missing piece
I thought I was made of more
I hope there is something I was made for
I am as large as an ocean when I think of others
I am growing as a person when I notice their struggle too
When I fade the dark color of their blue
Yet, I shrink to a pebble when I become self obsessed
Ignoring the bad habits that should be addressed.

The puzzle contains things that I enjoy
A cheerful feeling, like an infant with a toy
Putting on headphones and shutting my eyes
Listening to music is something I advise
Tying my cleats as I sit on the side, oh, how Soccer makes my mouth grin wide
Scoring a goal fills me with pride, and helping my teammates when they need a guide
My parents have always taught me to be a leader
To chase my dreams and to find my missing piece.

But puzzle pieces don't magically appear
So I have to keep searching for my beautiful ending
The journey to complete the puzzle is quite the adventure
Starting at the border, chasing the center
Too many pieces to count with their own story
I am a 5000 piece puzzle, searching for my missing inventory.

Category C, Individual Poem Grades 7–8

CARRIE P. WEBER MIDDLE SCHOOL
Mr. Burke, Grade 8

Healing a Tree
Isabelle Rubino

I am tired, tired is she
Who laughs all day,
And cries all night.
Each day starts the same,
As each day is the same.
Yet I am not.
I have grown and changed
As the bud of a flower
Grows and changes.
I was uprooted from birth,
And was handed off
To a new tree.
Families change they say,
They change and evolve.
But are they supposed to break,
I ask.
Are they supposed to break
Like a twig off a tree?
Can a tree heal after
lt's broken and destroyed?
I have to heal the tree,
I have to tape the twig,
I have to water the roots.
I am tired, tired is she
Who heals a home
And is forced to change.

MOUNT SINAI MIDDLE SCHOOL
Mrs. Wallace, Grade 8

My Name
Koharu Sato

My name

Always read and said wrong
The slight pause during roll call
The looking around the room to find
The person who owns it
I know it's me

My name

Given nicknames
Complimented
Gossiped
So unusual that when I hear it
I know it's me

My name

Shows the culture
Shows the race
Shows what I am
Yet people make fun of it
I know it's about me

But my name

So beautiful like the cherry blossoms
So warm like the meaning of the beginning of spring
So strong and mighty like the great mountain
So kind and sweet when my loved ones call
And when they do
I know it's me

My name

MANHASSET MIDDLE SCHOOL
Mrs. Pellegrino, Grade 8

Unaware
Jacob Torczyner

Though it may look like I am one,
Forced down under the pressure of failure,
I am truly many ones,
Sucked into a single trailer.

My traits abound, fight for first,
Looking for their chance to appear
Though their efforts are seemingly futile
To one that may look for a big appearance in a movie reel.

At my core rests one little trait,
Not affected or aware of truth's battle in the mind,
Living its life in peace and quiet,
Yet has never been defined.

If many personalities are needed,
In order to express my feelings,
A fight breaks out in my head,
Trying to figure out what I had just said.

There are times, though, that change the pace
Like a blank piece of paper in front of my face.
The purest form of expression I have found,
Right next to the drums that my patterns expound.

Though the writing might become messy,
The drums sounding like a stampede of nothingness,
Only the contradictions and mistakes show,
The truest trait in the core.

It is willing to fail, to mess up, to learn
From anything wrong expressed from the actions,
That the traits control from in the mind,
Yet the young trait is still confined.

This aspect known to all yet never much used,
The simplest elucidation of this attribute is growth, always mused.

Category C, Individual Poem Grades 7–8
HEBREW ACADEMY OF LONG BEACH
Ms. Toumazatos, Grade 8

Reflection
Valerie Torres

Shine as *bright* as a star
The quiet daisy standing in a field of sunflowers
My petals strive to bloom
Determined to put one foot in front of the other
No matter what
Step by step
Never looking back
Although my path is bumpy
I navigate the right direction
Afraid of the real world
What fantasy am I living in?
I look at my reflection
Struggling to define my true self
Picking out each puzzle piece
Every one is a flaw
The strangely **perfect** image
Is nothing like the inside
Just like a bird
I spread my wings
Watch them flutter
I fly *free*

The Multitudes
Oliver Won

Part I: The Soil, Air, and Rain,
From the ground to the sky,
From the east to the west,
I grow, I grow, I grow...
And because I was planted into the soil
Lived from the air
And fed from the rain
I became a listener to a speaker
From a defeat to a quest
I grew, I grew, I grew...
And because I was born into love
Lived from the care
And fed from the work
I became a loner to a brother
From Manhattan to Long Island
I grew, I grew, I grew.

Part II: The "shouldn't have happened"
But if I wasn't locked from the trees and grass would I have gotten the chance to learn to write these bars and lines?
But if I wasn't limited to finishing in the short time would I have gotten the chance to prove with the stars and rhymes?
If I had prepared myself for the worst, would I ever have truly "prepared" for it? Would I know the downs and pounds that you put on, and know the endless questioning of
"Why me?"

Part III: I
I tend to procrastinate, I hate practicing, I always protect, I keep promises, I love performing,
But frankly, many do too
So I know that I don't just speak for myself, But I speak for many
I speak for people two, four, six, times older than me
I speak for people across the globe, or the neighbors down the block
I speak for people that will love, care, work, move, write, sing, and grow
I speak for people that have multitudes.

Category C, Individual Poem Grades 7–8
GREAT NECK SOUTH MIDDLE SCHOOL
Ms. Klein, Grade 8

小鸟和我

Nancy Yu

BIRD AND ME

飞啊飞啊飞啊走啊
那只鸟在空中翱翔
在高空飞翔
鸟和我一样
然而我们同时又不同
当我跑步时，
我感觉到我周围的空气
风感觉又冷又刺骨
当我跑步时，
我感觉到风
它把我推回去，
但当我奔跑时，我感到自由
像鸟一样自由
感觉像鸟儿一样自由
然而我们不一样
鸟儿在天空翱翔
人们紧贴地面
我们很相似
然而我们同时又不同

Fly, fly, fly, away
The bird soaring through the air
Flying high in the sky
The bird and me are the same
Yet we are different at the same time
When I run,
I feel the air around me
The wind feels cold and bitter
When I run,
I feel the wind
It pushes me back,
But when I run I feel free
Free as a bird
Feeling as free as a bird
Yet we are not the same
Birds soar through the sky
People stick to the ground
We are similar
Yet we are different at the same time

Category C, Individual Poem Grades 7–8
NEW HYDE PARK MEMORIAL HIGH SCHOOL
Mrs. Romero, Grade 7

INDIVIDUAL POEM, GRADES 9 & 10

Category D

Grand Champion

I Am
Ava Kuklis

"Who am I?"
Society awaits a presumably confident response
Collectively bound to a persona, a public image, a reputation, a stereotype
Disregarding spectrum based judgment, you are unknowingly, and uncontrollably perceived
Subject to being falsely translated, vision based judgments you can skew only at eye level

I am a body
Melodies that course through my veins, sound that dictates the beat of my heart
Playing strands of hair like guitar strings, the callus of picking, plucking, fingers
Feet settled above ever changing destinations and evolving terrain
Acrylic scars on arms stretched like canvas, my head painted by Pollock
A pupil of my mother, an iris of my father, a ring of conspiracy bombarding visions of realism

I am an image
Black converse bursting at the sole, my sock easily visible, laces that restrict blood flow
Ripped tights and denim layered beneath stains
The black t-shirts of indistinct bands, worn all too many times
Disguised in an army green cardigan
An identity seen only from an outer shell, little concern for what lies within

continued

I am a distance
Watch from afar, I, a dark, faded figure, a silhouette with blurry borders, think nothing of it
Step closer, clearer, yet insignificant I stand as a person like all
The narrowing space between constructs illusion of individuality, stare into my being
Dissect my imperfections as the gap come to a close, the good the bad the me
Close enough to reach, look but don't touch

I am a time
Birthed into admirable cluelessness, optimism, and innocence
Blind existence makes for malleable potential, fresh youth yet to be polluted by corruption
Growing to fill shoes meticulously crafted with high expectations by those without expectation
Newfound joy in judgment, seeing surroundings through eyes capable of viewing shortcomings
Age opens the blinds to reveal introversion, tormenting self-loathing injected by inheritance

I am incoherent, I am immense, I am immeasurable

Category D, Individual Poem Grades 9–10
WESTHAMPTON BEACH HIGH SCHOOL
Mrs. Schmieder, Grade 10

Grand Champion

house of cards
Rina Olsen

i am a house of cards. construct me, hear my dimensional whispers.
i shake/fall apart/sprawl on the table as you sort through the faces on those cards:
Ho Nansorhon, Chopin, Van Gogh, Hypatia, the fisherman i said hello to last weekend.
we all toast marshmallows with Boyle's flamethrower, playing faro.
i am them. they are me. interchangeable parts, invented by Eli Whitney who joins us.
the cards are folded into paper planes and i soar, like the airplanes cross-stitching
a burnt evening sky flecked with seagull calls. the airplane my parents met on. the airplane
embroidering white streamers in the infinite blue prayer. like the lines criss-crossing

my palm. each one offering a different permutation of a path in life
but i only get to choose one. and my ancestors pass around the flamethrower
to set their evanescent dreams ablaze, saying *we are the other permutations.*
you are the last one but you still get to hold us all in your hand.
press my hand against a window. see the lingering ghost on the glass.

continued

Category D, Individual Poem Grades 9–10
SAINT JOHN'S SCHOOL
Mr. Harmon, Grade 10

the ghost of my hand that holds the cards that i study with my eyes.
Asian eye/my mother's eye/slim brown eye. anglo eye/my father's eye/wide blue eye.
spades and clubs merge, spill out of their own bodies into hearts and diamonds. bleed.
on one side of the house is the Twinkie [*yellow outside, white inside*]
on one side of the house is the egg [*white outside, yellow inside*]
they face each other through the triangles of the house. they merge, as different as 3-D lenses
made of midnight fractals patched together like a stained glass window. shards of this
intergalactic cavity we call home. they merge, to make one whole.

i am a house of cards. shuffle me, hear my rippling laughter.
you know me as a deck of cards. but in my splendor
i house myself. i house you. i house the sky, the sea, the ground.
i house the turbulent rip current sloshing beneath my [egg/Twinkie] flesh.
i house history notes, palm readings, smoking marshmallows, soft afternoon rain.
i house leaky pens, silent flamethrowers, dissipating music notes.
i house lowercase letters and misplaced, punctuation. i house the black suit and the red suit.
i house myself. as a house, i am complete.

A mosaic
Anika Amin

A collage of broken
Finished projects
Of moments and memories
Of meetings and magic
A mixed-media metaphor for
Magnified irrelevancy and apple picking:
Taking what I want
And locking the door so tight
I forget the rain that sneaks through the kitchen window
And chills the house
I built myself up and
Tore myself down
Watching each time as the air pockets of you got bigger
As your face appeared more and more in the glue
As I continue to use the word you
I'm stuck together with you and glue too
A two-for-one deal
I'm a hopeless mess of hope
As I stumble over my feet calling it a dance
And my tears won't run
So I have to
Pulling in every person and character and story I can't quite love
So when I break open
I fill myself
With just enough empty space not to sink
And then drown in my own eyes long enough to breathe

Paper Cranes
Hannah Bahn

They say the apple doesn't fall far from the tree, instead
it stays, ripening over time. It seems to be a minimal &
unbridgeable distance between person and person,

person and mind. Supplementing a lacking memory
with *Where do stars go during the day?* With the hindsight
of *things I should've asked & funny things*

I thought of only after we went silent. Repeatedly
reminding yourself of memories so they never vanish
and become the list of what's left, reinventing

themselves daily, placing new emphasis upon
tone of voice or the shakiness of a hand. Clinging
to the honeyed purple pain of *You know it's no longer there*

but you cherish the memories as if they weren't just the past
but the present and future, too.
Conjuring up magic tricks that memory and the moment

make sweeter, tracing the unsure folds of a paper wing or beak
then flattening them with a fingernail, memorizing
how the paper feels in your hands.

Love via a sense of longing, love
via a sense of never letting go

Me, Moment
Sophia Bergeron

I am everything that's happened to me, I am mixed up in a ball
I cannot find words for single notions- I'm afraid I'll use them all

I'm warm water in the kitchen sink after long hot showers
I'm my mother's fat cucumbers with their tiny yellow flowers

I'm a forty-year-old movie that I failed to comprehend
I'm the way that every month I succumb to the latest trend

I'm the young girl at my fifth grade table trying not to yawn
I'm the half-hour spent cleaning my room just before the dawn

I'm the song that reminds me of the friend that I miss the most
I'm the big stall in the school bathroom haunted by a ghost

I'm my father's auntie's daughter's cousin's mother's uncle's sister
I'm the moment in the deep night when I really wish I'd kissed her

I'm the buttons I spilled in the hallway before the world shut down
I'm the potholes freckling every road of my sad old hometown

I'm the dark green crew neck sweater that she never let me borrow
I'm the late due date in English class,
but I'll finish it tomorrow.

Sister
Colleen Carroll

I am a sister
I am a loyal listener, a best friend
The ear that heard you when no one else´s would
I am the little child playing with you in the glowing sun
I am your faithful friend running with you through the fields of youth
I am the frightened kid hiding in your room from the thunderstorm
I am the girl in a deep sleep on your shoulder
I am the girl that watched you grow older
The one who accompanied you throughout your childhood
The one who is still next to you walking along this winding road

But now our roads are farther apart
Stretching like a never ending rubber band
You have gone off to college leaving me behind
I am the girl who walks past your dark deserted room where we used to laugh for hours
I am the child who weeps without your helping hand
I am the dog awaiting his owner's arrival home, waiting for the sweet sound of the tires against the gravel
I am a ship in the empty sea
Until you come home
And the shimmering sun returns to the sky and the earth begins to turn again
Our house is a puzzle and you are the missing piece
I am the flower that only blooms in your presence, in your laughter, in your warmth, in your light
I am a sister

Category D, Individual Poem Grades 9–10

EASTPORT-SOUTH MANOR JUNIOR-SENIOR HIGH SCHOOL
Ms. Martin, Grade 10

Unabated Passion… Multitudes 2023
AnnaBelle Deaner

Birthed from agnostic parents of religious skepticism, my mother Catholically strict in disposition,
> Her reticence and miserliness, a remnant of prior generations of irrefutable indigence.

My dad, Jewish by descent, inspired by ardent cultural convictions;
> self-identification is a vibrant part of his spirit, as the legacy of the Holocaust still haunts him

like a nefarious cloud of contempt, expunging halcyon memories of pristine innocence.
> I possess the visceral and cerebral depths of my Father and the artistic tendencies of my Mom.

Multitudes of disparate parts – questioning beliefs while toiling tirelessly for those without voice,
> I navigate language through etymological immersion and linguistic experimentation.

Vivo en un mundo definido por la incertidumbre y un odio aparentemente inmutable.
> Cathartic expression of the internal struggles of protagonists; my passion lies on the proscenium.

Taking center stage as Matilda at the Engeman Theatre, I express the suffering of the disenfranchised.
> My 4'11" takes on the physical and emotional form of the multi-layered characters I portray.

My seemingly frail frame deceptive as I belt a high C with zealous ferocity.
> A child burdened by familial strife and the cacophonous resonance of discordance.

Counterbalanced by the deep undertones and harmonic rhythms of viola improvisation.
> Genetic markers combined with activated illness culminate in a diagnosis of Celiac.

continued

Dietary restriction, while limiting, propels me to greater heights of an unwavering commitment.
> Food Pantry Partner, Collective action galvanized through community action,

providing unlimited access to provisions for impoverished individuals with food allergies.
> Aspiring Environmentalist, Recycle Specialist, Organic Garden Cultivator and Overseer,

My collective selves, all incapable of surrendering to the offensive stagnation of the status quo.
> Empiricist, in the vein of Lise Meitner, persistent in placing science over personal accolades,

Penning prose through a lens of angst tempered by a selflessness of spirit.
> Vocalist, Violist, Scientist, Insatiably Curious Environmentalist, Leader, Embracer of Change,

Self-doubt juxtaposed against principled confidence, Compulsive action driven by unfettered love.
> Resilient I stand, unperturbed by external judgment, I represent all these selves simultaneously

and stand at the forefront of individuality with a genuine desire to unswervingly advocate.
> The lessons I have learned a reflection of the existence I have inhabited.

My impassioned teachers, friends, and parents all metamorphosize, embodying the spirit that fuels me,
> Unabated passion inextricably linked to my DNA; I fully embrace unity of spirit and purpose.

Ink, Coffee & Postage Stamps
Giuliana DePaola

A part of me is made of ink,
I've never been without a story.
I've told them, I've read them, I've written a few,
For without them I fear life is boring.

A part of me is a postage stamp,
Longing to reach every inch of the globe;
To see all there is with no cares in the world,
For regret is the worst thing I know.

A part of me is black coffee,
Bitter and dark to the core.
My mind warps despair into a puzzle to solve,
It sounds quite odd, I'm sure.

Sometimes I'm all of these things;
Sometimes I'm none,
Yet the strange combination
Is what makes life so fun.

I chase all the mysteries—
They inspire my writing,
Collecting adventures
Is all too exciting

Ink and coffee and postage stamps,
As outlandish as it gets;
But remove one of these pieces from me,
And I would simply cease to exist.

Category D, Individual Poem Grades 9–10
FLORAL PARK MEMORIAL HIGH SCHOOL
Grade 9

To Know You, Is to Know Me
Isabella Fernandim

To braid each other's hair, is to know youth
The ties of tradition
Sewn into each strand
Red ribbons falling loose

To paint the ceiling, is to know the sky
The boundaries of childhood walls
Turn off the light
Reach for the moon we created

To love you, is to know those before me
A mother's word of tongue
Strangers foreign songs
A mosaic of all the places I have ever belonged
Embrace me like the branches of our family tree

To know a mother, is to know a daughter
Your practices, my hands
We fight, we dance
The invisible rhyme of interwoven love

To know you, is to know me
The blood of memories flowing like waves
Let it ebb into the sea from our veins
They splash against the house love built
Wash away the marks of the burden you carried
Only to find they are mine to inherit

To know me, is to know you

Category D, Individual Poem Grades 9–10
SACRED HEART ACADEMY
Mrs. Rossi, Grade 9

Home
Anelisa Fulgieri

Home. Home is a noun that is defined by Merriam-Webster as "the social unit formed by a family living together". Plot twist: home is never one place. May 2, 2007: a baby girl was born in Mazatenango, Guatemala. Plot twist: her home would be inconsistent for a while. Little did this baby girl know that her birth mom could not raise a healthy child and provide a safe and loving life for one. May 6, 2007: the little girl was named "Rosa" by her birth mom. Plot twist: she was taken from the hospital by her mom and sent to live with a foster family in another part of Guatemala. Question: would she ever see her birth mom again? Answer... For the next seven months, Rosa would live with this foster family. Plot twist: she would move once more. May 16, 2007: a married woman in New York in the United States would receive a phone call stating that a Guatemalan girl was waiting to be adopted. This woman immediately rushed to her husband's job to deliver this news. Within weeks the married couple would arrive in Guatemala to meet their new baby girl. Over the next seven months, the couple would travel to Guatemala to bond with their future daughter. December 22, 2007: Rosa arrived at her new home in the United States. Plot twist: her name was changed. December 22, 2007-present: "Rosa" became Anelisa Grace Rosa Fulgieri. Although Anelisa's home changed frequently in the early months, she would learn to appreciate each one of her homes in a different way.

American
Emilin George

It started looking at the stars,
Laying in blades of grass, sitting in the trees,
or swinging on the tough rubber of an old beat up tire
Another kid in a small square house,
In a small square neighborhood,
In a small square town

I would look up at my mother and ask who we were,
And she would tell me tales of the hot Indian sun and the shade of palm trees,
Stories of struggle and triumph and unlikely victories,
Stories of how we earned our place here, our life, our home
When they asked who I was I would know
A gentle flower from rough roots

Then came the wind
The same but different
The same wind that gave me wings when I played on the swing,
Carried voices whose weight grounded me again, an unlikely enemy

Home became apparently unapparent
It seems I wasn't as American as I thought
I ran around the same playgrounds, biked around the same streets, caught fireflies in the same alleyways
But it will never be the same kind of home for me as it is for them
The home of my childhood stories became a fantasy land
The world faded, the memories lost
To them, I was nothing more than a familiar stranger.

The Beauty of the World
Isabella Gonzalez

Seated at my desk, I find that the lights, fluorescent,
are all that I ever needed. *I don't need to get up and
go*; the work packets staggered along the wooden
surface are essential in keeping me busy.

Confined in a four-walled room, with no windows
to be found, this is my sanctuary. The room, painted
in pale colors leaves my brain *unstimulated*,
molding me into a *mindless zombie*.

The fluorescents, illuminating the classroom, bring a
pounding to my head. The ceiling, my heaven, tells
me of the work I must produce. Deadlines are to be
met, tests are to be studied for. Work. Work. Work.

On my ride home, my head, against the window
shakes in rhythm with the bus. Boom.Boom.Boom.
The sun distracts me. I never noticed how the sun
stroked the blades

of grass that illuminate lime green rays, similar
to an emerald. The sky, covered in an array of dancing
sapphires, revealed the whimsy of cirrus clouds.
My eyes twinkled, growing a sense of admiration for the

beauty of the world. When's the last time you've
indulged in the fresh air provided by our mother earth?
Inhaling and exhaling. Have you sat in the grass?
Allowing yourself to become grounded: one with the earth.

LONG BEACH HIGH SCHOOL
Mrs. Koegel, Grade 10

Girl of Sand
Cate Grady

I find that as I grow older
I become more and more like a grain of sand,
Constantly mixing with others
and changing from new experiences
To become a slightly altered version of the same starting point
There are billions of others that could look just like me from the surface,
But every single one of us is on life's beach with our own stories to tell
For instance, the wind brought my family to this beach
from Ireland many years ago, but the grain next to me may have been just washed up from Hungary
but we erode with each other even if it is just for a short moment
so that the next place we end up
we will have made an impact on each other.
My tiny grain is composed of elements from far and wide:
the blue eyes passed down to me from my mother and her mother before her,
and my dark hair that sets me apart from them all.
Though seemingly insignificant, every act I make throughout my day has been influenced by my past;
my sense of humor, for example
was given to me by my father, but sometimes I see
him rubbing off on those close to me
There have been times where my grain has become rough and sharp to the touch
after being whipped around by life's oceans,
but when combined with the right people
I soften out again.
I, like all others,
am simply a girl of sand waiting to be washed away again
Hopeful to become a miniscule but unique
Part of a new castle

Even Blue Has Multitudes
Rachel Ha

Something old, something new, something borrowed—
Heirlooms of an immigrant daughter's grit,
And the "good bones" that've remained in the homes of our half-battered hearts—
                    Grandpa told us to stop painting all our woes blue.
 He threw the seeds onto this fertile land of opportunity,
Praying that Vietnamese heritage could prosper on this earth Americana.
My family tree is a humble oak that has kept me grounded,
Entwining me in roots so deep, it has grown past a bedrock bottom.
                                      Because even
Though you can grow, never forget from where you came.
My mother and father, both Vietnamese immigrants,
Traveled across
                                        turquoise seas
To put at least a penny to their name. Vowing to each other
Before I was born that they would crawl out of this hellhole
Called life and raise their children in the botanical gardens.

Born in Brooklyn but soft as the suburbs,
Since the second I came into this world my mother said that I loved to sleep—
But I'm not a dreamer, I'm a fighter, a denier, the kerosene
To forest fires because in spite of my acid tears
I burn to be better—learning to do so without scorching
The person I used to be into complete ashes.

I burn to find my own center, thinking twice before
Pulling myself into the concentric rings of fair-weather friends,
Whose axis I pivot in the splendor of fluorescent suns   **and cyan skies,**
But disappear in the eye of a hurricane.

In the eerie darkness, I look toward my grandpa, the guiding star,
Mom and dad, who defied gravity to make planets align,
In my orbit of an incandescent love that has the strength to tilt galaxies,
The people we cherish are the people we become, with
All individualities binded in solar systems that
                                        have great multitudes.

HERRICKS HIGH SCHOOL
Mr. Mattson, Grade 9

Jew(ish)
Isabella Kohl

I am from potato kugel
From stale rye bread and watered down grape juice
From hushed prayers over the dim candle light
and eating everything on the plate, even the brownest of bananas

I am from seders with grandparents
and "small get-to-gethers" with all my cousins that I didn't know I had

But I am not from kosher meals,
Or from butter alternatives
I enjoy shrimp, crab, and other shellfish

I am not from kissing the mezuzah before entering a room
I am not from fluency in my sacred text - far from it though I wish

I am not from the girls you read about in your history textbook
From keeping alive the ancient traditions
Or even from demonstrating them myself
I am not from the kind of Jew my ancestors would recognize

But I am from farina with dark chocolate chips
From stealing secret sips of my father's Manischewitz on Passover

From hamantaschen, latkes, and matzah ball soup
I am from late sunrise synagogue visits and early sunset breakfast dinners (*shana tova*)

I am also from occasionally forgetting to cover the challah before reciting the kiddush (*Baruch ata Adonai, Eloheinu Melech ha-olam, boreh p'ri hagafen*)

But I am from fighters
I am from survivors
I am from heroes who had strength and pride in their religion

And I am proud too
I am not the perfect Jew - I will do more
I will work to honor my religion and my ancestors
And I know they are proud of me
For, I am from forgiveness (*slicha*)

TRANSLATIONS
Shana tova - good year (traditional greeting for the jewish new year)
Slicha - sorry (asking for forgiveness)
Baruch ata Adonai, Eloheinu Melech ha-olam, boreh p'ri hagafen - Blessed are You, LORD our God, King of the universe, Who creates the fruit of the vine (blessing over the wine)

ROSLYN HIGH SCHOOL
Mr. Segal, Grade 10

Spear of Summer Grass
Caitlin Lee

I do not yet know who I am or what I'll become.
What is the grass?
How am I ever going to stand out from all the other blades…

The feeling of being not good enough,
Like an imposter inhabiting my own skin.
Needing to cut, cut, cut, through the standards of today,

Yet continue to grow, grow, grow,
Growing up
But growing too close to the sun.

But I'm trying.
Trying to celebrate my feats,
And touch the stars instead of getting burnt by the light.
Accepting who I am and recognizing my triumphs,
That I'm worthy of my accomplishments, big or small.

Valuing my achievements,
And learning to deserve my successes.
Growing tall and proud of who I'm meant to be.

Category D, Individual Poem Grades 9–10
HERRICKS HIGH SCHOOL
Mrs. Barnard, Grade 10

All and More
Julia Milos

I am a pencil.
I create lines, shapes, and shadows,
Then a picture.
I am a boat.
I bask in the light of the horizon, and float,
Then glide along the waters.
I am a calculator.
I scan through problems, analyze their data,
Then solve them.
I am a human.
I feel emotions, make mistakes, garner achievements,
Then repeat.
Artist,
Sailor,
Numerist,
Human.
I am all, and I am more.

Jazve[1]
Vladamir Mkrtchian

I remember the days warmly. The *jazve* singing
as my mom stood there like a tree. Like a tree,
her roots fixed on the pale wood floor,
as the wind slammed its expanse on the cool window;
these days were warm, like the sable storm she beckoned from the pot,
falling and glutting in a tiny cup.

These were the days I remember,
head perched on her bough while she sipped and singed. Her songs intertwined
with the inquisitive winds, and the questions rolled off my tongue,
falling as milk and sugar in her ceramic demitasse, still too bitter for me to drink.
Our chats rivaled colloquies; we chanted on and on
about a life of living under a pale roof, over pale floors,
while drinking black coffee.

Ten years later, I tower over the *jazve*; I let her sit
and wait for her share. This time
I'm her tree; I sway, stir, and pour into our new porcelain cups. Ten years later,
I stir milk and sugar in my coffee, but it's still too bitter for me to drink; I tightrope walk
down pale floors double-fisting shades of bark in pale cups, and lay them
down on the table. Ten years later, she's the one who asks about my day and school;
ten years later, she waits for me as I stir, sway, and pour
myself out to a life outside of pale roofs and off of pale floors,
but not without black coffee.

Twenty years later, we won't have coffee together every day, but
we'll wait together, we'll wait
for the days to ebb and flow along like small black sips. Twenty years later,
I limp over the rusty *jazve* and brew. I don't need milk or sugar;
I sway, stir, and pour alone. Twenty years later, every day grows icier, but
the ebony expanse of my branches kindles home; twenty years later,
the Ethiopian coffee grounds speak for you, gracing my chalky cup, piling
    and painting a past of
a life under pale roofs, over pale floors, and drinking black coffee.

---

[1] (jahz-veyh) a small metal pot, usually of copper, with a long metal handle, used for preparing Armenian-style coffee

Category D, Individual Poem Grades 9–10
WELLINGTON C. MEPHAM HIGH SCHOOL
Mr. Grosskreuz, Grade 10

Memories of Mine
Ariana Muhammad

I am large; I contain multitudes.

I am chunky hooped earrings, sterling silver disguised in shimmering gold.
I am summertime strawberry farms and ice-cold grape Fanta,
From the roaring ceiling fan and ornate Mediterranean carpet in my living room.

I am the gentle breeze of the sandy sea shore.
I am late nights and early mornings, a dreamer from dusk till dawn,
From Fourth of July camping encounters with masked raccoons, and New Year's Day brunches.

I am singing to Bieber with my cousins as we drive down Interstate Ninety-Five South.
I am inky eyelashes with a Cheshire Cat smile,
From clean piles of dirty laundry, desperately longing for the washing machine.

I am deep fried coconut shrimp drizzled with lime and red chili peppers.
I am shoulder-length, sunbaked hair, soaring wildly as I dance alone against the wind,
From Friday afternoon prayers and intricate henna tattoos on the eve of Eid.

I am peace and anxiety, my moods shifting quicker than a hungry lioness in the savannah.
I am "sisters stick together no matter what,"
From the passing of my graceful great-grandmother, the image of her sipping sweet tea in a hammock engraved in my mind.

I am candid photographs with childish captions glued into a scrapbook.
I am Long Island, and Pakistan, and Kenya,
From Farina and Amir, to whom I owe everything.

I am large; I contain multitudes.

NEW HYDE PARK MEMORIAL HIGH SCHOOL
Mr. Colvin, Grade 9

Bulletproof Legacy
Rizwan Rumi

King Rumi, a Gigachad from Grindset City
Fearsome man so devastatingly dangerous to society
Society and government shall put no hands on me
Indeed they have no control over the rebellious

An individual who dares to be different
Who strives to go against the norms of society
I'm the star that brings brightness to the dark sky

Indeed I'm a man who's feared by everyone
My power has gone out of control
My dominance is felt by the most elite

Rumi is more than just a name, its acronym stands for
    Resistant, Unstoppable, Magnificent and Inspiring

Man resistant to all sorts of changes
Man so unstoppable his dreams cannot be destroyed
Man is so magnificent, he can take over any nation within milliseconds
Man has inspired millions, he has dared to walk a different path

They chase for A's while I chase for money
They scroll through TikTok while I read books
They slide in her DMs while I connect with God
They work for money while money works for me
They invest in liabilities while I build my assets
They party while I'm at the gym
They wait for vacation while everyday of my life is a vacation

A man so rich, Elon Musk feels broke when he sees my wealth
I'm as fast as the speed of light, I am like a diamond I shine, I don't break
I'm dangerous, I repeat I am so dangerous, I'm a lightening I'm ready to strike
I'm am not your average Joe

You don't wanna feel my wrath I promise
None shall program me into believing in false truth.
My confidence cannot be destroyed neither it can be repeated by any one else
Brace yourself, I'm ready to take over

Category D, Individual Poem Grades 9–10
NEW HYDE PARK MEMORIAL HIGH SCHOOL
Ms. Sansotta, Grade 10

Goldfish
Natalia Sanchez

I am pretty to look at—
I have rouge scales and bulbous eyes
I swim in circles every morning,
and every night too.
I am the only one in my sweet abode,
but I can see other people with a blurry view.

You tap ten flakes into the top—once every day,
You tap my glass and you laugh
You stare and you sigh
You don't think about the things the way I do.

I am gentle and thoughtless;
I swim, I swim, I swim.

But I can remember things for more than a few seconds.
I remember how you made me feel last Tuesday,
when you left me all alone,
I remember the chilling breeze when you walked away.

I don't remember a time when I was not your goldfish,
and I dread how I can't recall the memory—
But I know I am not yours,
I am my own goldfish.

Unheard Melody
Ashna Shah

And as I ran away from the fearsome dog, I tripped and fell on my own foot - my own self - causing me to fall
But a bandage was placed so secure, contrasting brightly against my brown skin
And as I stood back up with no other legs but mine, I held the sugar cane that my mother had given me

Pouring more and more sugar from it into my chai, I filled it up so it could be as sweet as the me inside
And going deeper and deeper inside, every cell building tissues, every tissue building me slowly
All elaborately coded by the DNA made before me
But not a single strand could tell people enough about me, it couldn't code all of me
It needs others, it needs more, to even remotely make up a fraction of my worth

Or so I thought, as I watched others laugh at my display of weight, and foreign culture they couldn't comprehend

And as a mighty heart picks between good or bad, the sky too picks between the sun and moon
And it's times like these that I wonder how the atmosphere can be so brave, even with fireworks exploding inside

So as I play the same melody I always have, since I am opposed to change
Moving my left hand on the frets of the ukulele
I start to strum a new tone, one that I've never done
Because who knows
Maybe I'll like the new, as much as I like the old

A Long Way to Go
Siddhanth R. Surya

I am caramel swirls and sable curls,
warm apple pie served with cardamom masala chai
in chipped mugs older than I am.
I am fireworks that burst and bloom and sizzle
in the twilight on the Fourth of July and on Diwali.
I am the grace of an eagle and the pride of a peacock,
soaring, strutting, singing, putting on a show.
I am the strings of a spruce violin and the chords of a teak sitar,
pulled and plucked in solitude when the world is too much to bear.
I am the rainbow hues of oil paints, and the fragrant heaps of Holi *gulal*,
unfolding like a vibrant tapestry, woven witness to human tales.
I am black and white films watched on rainy Friday evenings,
and charcoal drawings scribbled into creased sketchbooks;
comforting restless hearts and pensive minds.
I am kind brown eyes with wrinkles dancing in the corners,
and chafed pink hands, toiling to nourish and sustain.
I am hearty belly laughs that bounce off walls decorated with regal portraits,
and salty tears that make puddles on dust covered scrapbooks.
I carry the richness of two worlds within my soul, my blessing and my burden;
but I still have a long way to go.

Category D, Individual Poem Grades 9–10
NEW HYDE PARK MEMORIAL HIGH SCHOOL
Mr. Colvin, Grade 9

If I Were Free
Jaclyn Xue

If I were set free,
I would dance myself to the doors of heaven,
Twisting and twirling,
Clothes flapping in the warm breeze,
Feet tapping gently on soft grass,
Hand in hand with my mother's fiery essence.
I would follow the sweet simmering notes of a faraway place,
Running to drown in its purity,
Brimming with its emotion,
Losing myself in the brilliance of my father's musical hands.
I would bask in the warmth of the bright yellow sun,
And soak its heat into every breadth of my skin,
Bringing me back to childhood's doting paradise,
And days of laughter with my sister's daring spirit.
I would smell the succulent notes of my grandma's stove,
Her recipes melting inside my mouth,
Sweet and sour and bold,
Warming me from the inside with her gentle love.
If I were set free,
I would see the whole world
And be filled with endless multitudes.

INDIVIDUAL POEM, GRADES 11 & 12

Category E

Grand Champion

Traveling Pots
Hannah Ninan

We are clay, molded to portray living breathing humans
Questioning our existence on a planet out in nowhere
Still made with a purpose-
Perfectly purposely sculpted
As the universe came together to create each one of us.
But those small dents, the exaggerations the sculptor makes - we are those flaws
If we all were perfect, I wonder if we won't need names 'cause we are one,
Molded from the same clay.
Handing over our brokenness, worries, and pressures, to someone out there
To be handed back a beautiful mosaic depicting a story of gold.
We turn into pots carrying golden memories
Together grasping pots of gold we walk on,
Feeling useless but told we are made for greatness.
We carry on to our own rhythm, experiencing a story
None in the billion years of Earth have experienced.
In this pathway, we try to learn the stories of others,
Crossing buildings that hold the minds that could have soared over clouds
 like kites.
Mercy crosses the pink stained glass building
Through which the grandness of the illuminations falls on the faces of sinners.
We go through the highs and lows of life, waiting in line to become stable,
So to finally rest in peace and be happy in solitude.
Sweet solitude, like an oasis
Though we crave solitude,
In multitudes, we are born, we walk, we die.
Though seasons change, our fight doesn't seem to stop,
We fight together to endure the coldness of our hearts and the heat of our minds.
Fighters, we are, fighting that these rains and storms don't deform us.
Though death brings peace, we fight to make it out happy with our way of life.

Category E, Individual Poem Grades 11–12
NEW HYDE PARK MEMORIAL HIGH SCHOOL
Ms. Kaspar, Grade 12

Grand Champion

sixth period
Rainer Pasca

the boys' bathroom smells like
chemicals and smoke
and i am in a gravestone of life
i am waiting for the fire alarm to ring
spray me with the holy water on the floor
refresh me with the sense of the high school
where am i in this moving set piece
where do i fit in here
or is this desk simply too small for me
the crushed vape pen on the floor
is still fuming, still waiting
for someone else to submit to the galaxy
handing over fate for the gods of detention
kiss me with your breath
it smells like corporate greed
lock the door and turn down the lights
mop the floor and start a fight
you are waking up slowly
and when you realize that we are all dust
i wonder where all that gravitas will go
i wonder where all the slurs you use will go
i wonder how your thoughts will dissipate
into gasses infused with nicotine
and i wonder just how many birds
they will kill in the process

BAY SHORE HIGH SCHOOL
Mr. Iannello, Grade 12

Burn Scars
Lyla Forest Butler

My mom talks about the dust, mostly
the after. Right now is after.
She doesn't like to think of people
she'd exchanged words with, people whose
careful arrangements of our alphabet she'd swallowed–
She doesn't like to think of people
whose heartbeats she'd held a couple of, heartbeats that no longer
shake those ribcages, that no longer stand guard like the frame of a building–

She doesn't like to think of those people
as ashes in the east river, leftover cremation.
people she knew now rest in the bottom of my city-kid lungs. i've grown up
breathing in their ashes, my own lungs pink & sweet, virgins to fire & smoke.

they live in us instead of in
their little studio apartments or their parents' house.
all burned– something untamable. it was a wild elephant–
my mom loves elephants.
her mind's eye is a menace, but it bites at her hand when the hand picks up a pen,
so i try to transcribe the sound of her thoughts–
big flames, children & elevators,
tvs that shut everyone up the way a good blizzard does,
airplanes, ashes, downtown ground.

She talks about lines down the block
she'd waited in for hours with her friends
to give blood to people
in a deadly silent city, that same city that never sleeps.
they thought people would need blood
so the lines snakes in thousands up the avenues–

lines down the block
to give blood to ghosts–
ghosts whose bodies we breathe.

This Is All You Need To Know
Lyla Forest Butler

I tried to go back home, but the trees
that had once coughed out
a border green & sacred,
were gone: a puff of thin smoke.
There was a little brook I'd follow
home, my hand dragging gently
in the cool, but I could only find
a snaking echo left there
a raisin of a dream.
The mountains that stayed
snow-capped through June
were now all washed in gray,
the birds that slept
in between the trees' fingers
were napping in some other barks.
I began to paint my shoes with
the dirt I'd known as a child, reckless
& joy-stained, but my breath
began to weigh me down:
some cloud of dark matter
flooded my lungs.
As I collapsed, I heard
the distant ring of familiar
sweetness: the voices of
children together.
But shouldn't they be in school?
They spoke of burning trees & hungry people,
no birds, no rain, no life.
I realized my home had evaporated.
The adults walked briskly past.

SAINT ANN'S SCHOOL
Mr. Skoble, Grade 11

Happiness
Luis Corvera

Happiness! It's in the front seat of my Porsche. Happiness is everywhere but my happiness is in this Porsche 911. My happiness it's found in the WASH, the DRIVE, the EXPERIENCE. The wash the lather of the soap dripping off the black paint, the BEAUTY engaging the world under the layer of dirt, the SHINE beaming brighter than the sun at noon. The drive...smooth as ever like if it was fresh off the lot pure twin turbo flat six engine sounds all eyez on me like Tupac said. 0-60 in 4.0 seconds i'm driving a rocket ship with wheels except it's very appealing to the eye. The EXPERIENCE pure happiness like never before a jolt of energy the urge to never get out. Seeing the world from a new perspective I'VE CONQUERED THE WORLD. Just me and my Porsche strolling for miles and miles onto the horizon. The experience will forever be my favorite. Flash back to reality now i'm done daydreaming gazing out the window back to my not so favorite part of the day sitting in my English class back to reading this boring novel.

UNIONDALE HIGH SCHOOL
Mr. Rinhauser, Grade 12

Terrible, just Awful
(People, not the poem itself)
Seth Del Orbe

People say we contain multitudes. Like, a bunch.
A bunch of multitudes, I mean.
I guess that's true. They'd have to.
How do terrible people have relationships?
Sorry for the swerve. It's just something I've been thinking about.
Like, I know sometimes people just share...views
but other times
they just put up with all the terrible
because maybe they see something we don't.
They're probably delusional
But hey! That's the multitudes.
(You can just imagine some sort of rimshot here maybe. if you wɛnt)

The Vine that Swallowed the South
Adelrhany Georges

My grandfather owned a cemetery,
swallowed completely by kudzu vine.
Every year I entered the flora entranced,
fascinated by how the leaves softened lines.

In a way, the stems resembled my grandfather,
perhaps they too took notice of his aging face.
In my moments of selective solitude, he would be there
grimacing and amused,
as the forest sounds imitated his gait.

Very soon the vines swallowed him as well.
The hard edges of his body softened green.
The walks into the famished flora grew more frequent,
and so were the faces impersonated by the leaves.

Kudzu vine is quite intrusive,
making an effort to listen as it preys and eats.
Each day I would see you in passing
faintly,
rooted firmly beneath my feet.

As I lay back on the supple slope of the land,
gazing up while cradled in your invasive arms.
Each leaf flashes a glimpse of myself,
as kudzu replaces the stars.

places visited
Queenie Liu

一片开满油菜花的田野	A field full of rapeseed blossoms
平坦,舒展	flat, stretch
童年的歌	childhood song
沿着小路在牛背上欢唱	Sing along the path on the back of a bull
炊烟在傍晚的青瓦上	The smoke from cooking is on the blue tiles in the evening
跳荡嬉戏	jumping and playing
谁家的采桑姑娘	Whose family's mulberry picking girl
挽起纱袖	roll up the sleeves
面对小河	facing the river
梳洗那甜蜜的梦境	Freshen up that sweet dream
来来往往	come and go
成群的,白色的	clustered, white
鸟儿们	the birds
在朝圣青春的衣裾	In the pilgrimage of youthful garments
老木屋里	in the old wooden house
一本静默的挂历	A silent calendar
高举双手	Raise your hands
仰望长空	looking up at the sky
祈祷令人惊喜的生命宣言	Pray for an amazing manifesto of life
古老的窗台上	on the old window sill
小小的洁白的茉莉花	The little white jasmine
轻轻芬芳了每一扇	Gently fragrance every door
紧闭的窗棂。	closed window lattice.

Burdens
Adelyn Loh

the maple tree does not like the birds.
too heavy, it screams, but the birds don't listen.
more come, stepping on its rough bark,
ignorant of the tree's cries.

the maple tree feels the hot, scorching sun,
and for a moment, the wind brings peace,
until little aliens with tiny hands,
climb up the bark, sending ripples of pain.
the tree moves slightly.
fazed, they stumble off, down the bark of the tree,
scraping their knees and crashing into the coarse, earthly soil.
the wailing of the aliens rings in the tree's ears,
pounding at its heart.
i'm sorry, make it stop.

the maple tree wants to stay green.
don't leave me, it whispers,
as each of the golden leaves lifts off the branches.
the tree tries to reach out and catch them,
before they drift to the ground,
but soon the tree is stripped bare, feeling so uneasy, so naked.
the wind feels crueler than usual against its coarse, earthly skin,
as the tree holds its arms closer to its chest.

the maple tree is numbed by the sharpness of the snow.
the snow will not leave, so its arms bend to hold it all,
arching closer and closer to the ground,
a kind of prayer for the sun.
please, take it all away.

the maple tree feels nothing at all, yet everything.
everything, all at once.

The War of Individuality
Paige MacPherson

The platform dissolves and the train won't
    come
When large-dark pupils unclick
 a head in heaven, toes untethered
 I close my lids and self simply gone

Quite often, self fits neatly in two boxes:
Self-ish, or less
A half-way self, or, simply none.
The surgeon general's recommendation
stands to be
none.
It's better for everyone that way.

But you
With your eyes
and your "I's"

Even I
God, I hate "I"
Ache to be more
than ish or less.

But do I want to
Hook my finger stalwart
behind my corneas
and pull til' pop.
Or do I only crave
the colors
that dance across
my sockets
in the dark.

Fluid
Candida Villalta Meza

Yo quisiera romper las cadenas (I wish I could break the chain)
Of splitting my culture into two.
Soy como el agua del Océano Pacifico (I'm like the waters of the Pacific Ocean)
I flow from one culture to another,
Lo hago sin esfuerzo. (I do it with no effort)

I am fluid, containing multitudes
Not sure what to call myself,
It's like an identity crisis.
It's like being a hypocrite.

What a Hypocrite I am
For wanting to be a whole.
Not a half or a quarter
I am a whole.

Like my ancestors, whole.
Independence, Confidence, Honesty
I strive to have multitudes.

Sky Lanterns
Allison Xu

When the night devours daylight,
frost edges the windowpanes
with pale blue tinges.
A feeling of isolation
curdles into suffocation.

We venture to the dirt clearing
that surrounds the ice-coated lake.
Chill closes over our shoulders,
bleeds into the crevices of our hair,
seeps into our toes.

Our hands cradle the silk paper shells
wrapped around the ring-shaped wire frames
and light the small burner sitting at the center.
A burst of illumination, the air inside
drenched in rich colors of persimmon.

We stand on tiptoe and fling our arms up,
releasing the sky lanterns,
watching them drift upward
with cooing sounds
like a flock of birds fluttering out of a cage.

Dancing, they pull against gravity and warm
the smothering darkness to studs of gold.
We strain our eyes to trace the waving glimmers
that wink and shrink into sparkly dots,
craving for the simple joy of freedom.

Multitudes
Emily Grace Zabala

Every mind consists of open doors, a room filled with worn out locks and withered wars—
Left to travel down roads of unfamiliarity.
Here one will easily become sore, bruised, and scorned.
Perhaps this is where my multitudes lie, behind the shy giggles and relentless internal wars—
I sit in serenity glancing at the stars and use my voice to share my ideas and infinite diminutive curiosities.
Presumably, my multitudes lie in fragmented memories or the fact that I am alive and have thrived.
Multitudes are the pieces of oneself that live behind tinted windows and tear stained pillowcases;
Behind the closed curtains of solitude placed besides the lies that have never survived.
The question is where they reside.
Perhaps I have it all wrong and my multitudes came from:
A shy guy who told me I chased a purpose driven high,
A mother who sacrificed her peace for the sake of my life,
A little girl who thought of me as gorgeous through her eyes,
And a song that opened my mind to live my life on a high- rise.
I remember that first feeling of being denied the ability to soar at blissful heights.
The contradictions of living a vast life, when thrown into the enclosure with all the social butterflies,
prideful lions, and enigmatic foxes who enjoy causing a fright.
I also remember running around my yard trying to fly a broken kite, learning about the intricacies of
flight, drinking cans of Sprite, and learning the "special phrases" I needed to highlight.

continued

It was never about the pages in the book that I could recall, but the details hidden in plain sight.
I now realize my multitudes are hidden in the silver lining of life such as—
Watching a family fight to stay alive, listening to my grandma romanticize the seemingly negative aspects of her life,
Determination of a young man to hear the heartbeat of his first child, and witnessing the human struggle to seek light.
Multitudes are fractions of others portrayed throughout our lives and the things that allow us to stay in the fight.
I had been looking at every imperfection in the mirror and never acknowledged my quirky personality, bubbly smile,
And lighthearted vows, my mismatched socks and purposeful days— living in the now, my perception of the world
And artistic capabilities, the way in which I listen to others and the imprint of their "highlighted phrases"
This is where my multitudes reside— in every fragment of light passing the restless nights.
I contain the multitudes of life, something bigger than I myself—
I sought— I found, a luminescence deep within my passionate cries and outcast might abound.

NEW HYDE PARK MEMORIAL HIGH SCHOOL
Ms. Kaspar, Grade 12

INDIVIDUAL ANTHOLOGY

Category F

Grand Champion

Tiny Allegiances
from Whispers Across the Fields
Christina Pan

Mom held my hand through the smoky streets, through the faceless drivers
    behind their unlit windows.
I skipped as she walked, reciting the tale of the monkey from school.
I dream of the day you can tell me your story in English, she said.

Lofty, I thought, like she told me to climb up to the clouds and
Invite the angels down to play gorillas in a tea party.

Giants walk the earth, walk past me, forever a third grader.
In my sleep I pledge my loyalty to my age, a patriotic third grader.
Yet every year my pledge changes, tacking on just another year,
Writing just another name, displaying just another photo.

My tongue faded while strange sounds came in as replacements.
My song, my poems, my letterbox, ripped from me slowly like

I was deaf to the tears of the pages until the pages are lost to the western winds,
Blown to oceans away, soaked, dissolved, its ink washing away.

CLASS ANTHOLOGY, GRADES 3 & 4

Category G

Grand Champion

Glitter Upon Mountains
Ms. Zucaro—3rd Grade Class
FORT SALONGA ELEMENTARY SCHOOL

Alivia Abbondondolo
Justin Auffermann
Isla Coiasi
Aiden Comparetto
Noah Diaz
Isabel Fuentes
Vincent Inforna
Emma Inserra
Noelle Kozub
Lucas Lindsey
Merida McDonald
Sabina Mikolajuk
Joshua Mushyakov
John Musso
Liam Pachacz
Samantha Szabo
Gavin Zeltmann

CLASS ANTHOLOGY, GRADES 7 & 8

Category I

About Us
Ms. Pomaro—8th Grade Period 2 Class
MOUNT SINAI MIDDLE SCHOOL

Zachary Bocker
Alanna Cappetta
Caylee Daderian
Kodye Dillon
Lyla Giarrizzo
Craig Hall
Savannah Hesse
John Horvath
Joseph L.
Alexandra L.

Kaila Marsala-Malin
Ryan Martin
Kylie Melendez
Ryleigh Nauronis
Connor Nicholas
Nolan Puccio
Madeline Ryan
Cristian Titone
Tyler West

A Multitude of Poems (Volume 1)
Mrs. Wallace—7th Grade Period 1 Class
MOUNT SINAI MIDDLE SCHOOL

Isabella Bustamante
Leah Caravello
Kevin Chartrand
Charlotte DeMouth
Layla Duran
Lucia Faldetta
Mikayla Ferguson
Evan Gippetti
Gabriella Grecco
Michael Han
Jake Imwalle
Madison Kelly
Natalie Malizia
Anna Mankuta
Ella-Marie Mazzara
Ryan McAuliffe
Devyn McMahon
Delaney Ramos
Giovani Schiavone
Lylah Sulpizio
Samantha Trypaluk

A Multitude of Poems (Volume 2)
Mrs. Wallace—8th Grade Period 2 Class
MOUNT SINAI MIDDLE SCHOOL

Hayden Ackerman
Ethan Arita
Jaxon Caruso
Leanna Dekenipp
Kadyn Dillon
Renelle Fields
Brody Gagnon
Azaan Iqbal
Alexander Katsaros
Alexander Latini
Geo Mangaran
Gianna Papa
Emma Ramos
Paisley Stoner
Sienna Westcott
Ava White

A Multitude of Poems (Volume 3)
Mrs. Wallace—8th Grade Period 3 Class
MOUNT SINAI MIDDLE SCHOOL

Gavin Birnstill
Gia Britt
Alex Brown
Alexa Cergol
Danny Chen
Lilly DeJesus
Nicholas DeVito
Leilani Dilone
Callie Friedman
Zoe Frisk
Olivia Genao
Daniel Hall
Mason Luckert
Thomas Massaro
Curtis Mellow
Brooke Mendelson
Jacob Mendelson
Aleks Niegocki
Sara Rahman
Salvatore Rao
Thomas Raic, Jr.
Capri Rienecker
A.J. Rode
Nicholas Teriaco
Abigail Tomay
Sofia Vardaro

A Multitude of Poems (Volume 4)
Mrs. Wallace—8th Grade Period 6 Class
MOUNT SINAI MIDDLE SCHOOL

Corinthea Carrion
Alex Contardi
Grace DeRosa
Matthew Fitzgerald
Christin Gale-Broere
William Glandorf
Alyssa Henderson

Jack Hermann
Venessa Idapalapati
Faith Jones
Savannah Kirschner
Samantha Kriedter
Max Lenz
Ryan McLaughlin

Jack Murphy
Sean Oakes
Joseph Perrotta
Isabelle Rubino
Nura Syeda
Hailey Trepiccione
Ella Woodruff

A Multitude of Poems (Volume 5)
Mrs. Wallace—8th Grade Period 9 Class
MOUNT SINAI MIDDLE SCHOOL

Kathryn Arrington
Simra Azim
Kendal Betro
Gianna Candurra
Samantha Epshteyn
Bella Falco
Gia Florio
James Haynes
Kayleigh Hegreness
Kyleigh Hertz

Malia Lockhart
Michael McFadden
Brandon Montalvo
Mahika Palukuri
Nikhil Patel
Addison Pescatore
Anthony Pramataris
Jackson Rannazzisi
Maiya Staudt
Alexandra St. George

Zachary Stone
Olivia Szczepanik
Senceria Tessler
P.J. Tubianosa
Nicholas Vaccaro
Lilianna West
Angela Zhang
Chelsie Zhao

Chapters of Life
Ms. Doran—7th Grade Period 3 Class
MOUNT SINAI MIDDLE SCHOOL

Dominic Angerame
Jake Bergold
Matthew Bram
Elly Chen
Gavin Hertz

Sebastian Lanning
Daniel McLoughlin
Frank Milicia
Aarav Penagaluru
Christian Quartaone

Leah Robert
Joey Stravino
Coraline Vertucci
Raymond Zheng

Everyone's Story
Ms. Doran—7th Grade Period 8 Class
MOUNT SINAI MIDDLE SCHOOL

Sofia Blednykh
Kenneth Brosdal
Joey Faby
Steven Godden

Nathanael Hart
Joshua Levine
Gianni Maola
Genevieve Miller

Peter Recupero
Vienna Rodriguez
Gia Turnquist

Listen to Who I Am
Ms. Doran—7th Grade Period 7 Class
MOUNT SINAI MIDDLE SCHOOL

James Acierno
Malia Ayala
Zahara Campos
James Casino
Raegan Chamberlain
Rey De La Cruz
Francesco Del Poeta
Jenna Elbahey

Nicholas Fazio
Lily Fusco
Jacob Gross
Eleanor Haas-Colwell
Jason Hayes
Emma Heins
Kian Karpinski
Kirill Kayran

Cailyn R. Lenz
Kyra Metzler
Travis Molomo
Sofia Perez
Luke Peterson
Max Snider
Dylan Zahra
Lily Zick

The Many Parts That Make Us Whole
Ms. Pomaro—8th Grade Period 9 Class
MOUNT SINAI MIDDLE SCHOOL

Antonio B.
Niko B.
Quintin B.
Annie C.
Carmine C.
Giselle D.
Iliana D.
Jeremy F.
Leon F.

Sophia G.
Graham H.
Brianna Javier
Doriya K.
Kyle L.
Brooke M.
Tyler M.
Dan P.
Lucas P.

Addisyn R.
Diana R.
Jeshua R.
Brandon S.
Caroline S.
Emma S.
Nick W.
Patrick Y.
Lizzie Z.

CLASS ANTHOLOGY, GRADES 9 & 10

Category J

Grand Champion

Multitudes of Us
Ms. Murphy—9th Grade Period 3 Class
OYSTER BAY HIGH SCHOOL

Riley Baehr
Mia Bencal
Matthew Cohen
Zoe Cohen
Julia DeAngelis
Scarlett Fredrickson
Sophia Gerbosi
Aryan Gumaste
Andrew Jennette
Giovanna Lisa
Giovanni Marinos
Dylan Nola
David Ortuno-Cabadiana
Giovana Sacco
Anya Schade
Ellia Stuart
Luka Verbanac
Emalyn Zeller

Beauty and Grass in All Things
Ms. Junjulas—Grades 9–10
MASSAPEQUA HIGH SCHOOL

Anthony Bennett
Ava Castillo
Archie Chesler
Ashley Crespo
Ava Geaniotis

Domi Gersbeck
Sienna Massimi
Gavin Ramos IV
Jake Rodriquez
Shira Shorr

Julianne Stainkamp
Kellsie Verdone
Kayla Viera

We Are Multitudes
Ms. Martin—10th Grade Period 6 Class
EASTPORT-SOUTH MANOR JUNIOR-SENIOR HIGH SCHOOL

Klever Lojda Aucapina
Griffin Becker
Ralph Betner
Colleen Carroll
Logan Delumen
Alyssa Didonna
Jessica Diers
Vanessa Gregorio-Lazaro

Luis Coxic Jax
Brandon Kern
Andrew King
Christopher Laguerra
Isabella Mazzochi
Chloe Schweers
Jasmine Taylor
Kendall Ward

Dylan Wayrich
Collin Wolters

CLASS ANTHOLOGY, GRADES 11 & 12

Category K

Grand Champion

Letters Unsent
Dr. Faughey—11th Grade Period 2 Class
OYSTER BAY HIGH SCHOOL

Nancy Abode
Jacob Albert
Ciara Barefoot
Deanna Besart
Leah Cerami
Peter Coschignano
Emma Curry
Christopher Dean
Olivia Gallo
Willy Henry
Oliver Keczmer

Joseph LaRosa
Sierra Nesis
Nicholas Ramirez
Kyra Sansone
Abygail Seslowsky
Giovanna Sherlock
Christopher Villegas
Marco Vlacich
Themie Voumvourakis
Jenny Yang
Matthew Zakarian

A Melodic Escape
Dr. Faughey—11th Grade Period 4 Class
OYSTER BAY HIGH SCHOOL

Franchesca Alejo
Sarah Byrne
Grace Curry
Ava DeAngelis
Jack DiFiglia
Jack Iocolano

Ania Kelly
Nicole Krumholz
Omek Kumar
Brooklyn Matt
John Purcell
Chiara Rutigliano

Joseph Sapienza
Sophia Sattar-Reiss
Gabriela Torres
Grace Yerkes

All Shapes and Sizes
Ms. Martin—11th Grade Period 5 Class
EASTPORT-SOUTH MANOR JUNIOR-SENIOR HIGH SCHOOL

Cole Alaimo
Ryan de Blasi
Anastasiia Bodnariuk
Elijiah Cater
Cameron Garcia
Danny Gershonowitz

Jennifer Ortiz Gonzales
Stephen DiLeone
Caelan Juliano
Grace Kral
Caitlin McGovern
Marcus Rivera

Delanie Satriana
Ivan Sintsov
Ayden Wefer
Christian Zambrano

I Encompass Worlds
Ms. Cho—11th Grade Period 2 Class
PLAINVIEW-OLD BETHPAGE JOHN F. KENNEDY HIGH SCHOOL

Hailey Acquaviva
Sari Bernstein
Claire Chai
Kyra Cheung
Connie Choi
Avani D'Souza
Aiden Gasbarro
Dylan Germain
Lindsay Hamburger

Morgan Hesekiel
Sunwoo Kang
Johanna Kim
Maya Kunis
Madison Laucella
Ilan Medwed
Josh Pudell
Ethan Recientes
Zachary Rosenberg

Ben Selmer
Maryam Shahid
Adam Stepansky
Cadence Tassone
Sofia Tsvetkova
Ivan Wu
Alex Zizzo

Versions of Myself
Ms. Cho—11th Grade Period 4 Class
PLAINVIEW-OLD BETHPAGE JOHN F. KENNEDY HIGH SCHOOL

Samantha Feldman
Samantha Graf
Steven Greenberg
Alexa Hakim
Sarah Han
Jacob Idy
Hannah Jung
Mackenzie Keichline
Shakoor Khairzada

Aanya Khandelwal
Sarah Khandelwal
Chloe Lam
Madison Lee
Eli Lev
Kangxi Li
John McNamee
Jacob Millman
Christina Pan

Marina Paraskevopoulos
Alex Reifer
Kyle Shum
Jesse Singer
Thomas Smith
Stella Toto
Gabi Weinstein

Multimedia

Category L

Grand Champion

My Hair That Makes Up Me
Malia Lockhart

My hair is a multitude of me.
My hair is chestnut brown like the mahogany Swietenia Macrophylla trees
That sway graciously in Africa.
My hair has kinky, curly strands that tell stories of their own.
My hair is a way to convey my instinctive state of mind.

I wear my hair as a crown,
A way to project myself abstractly rather than verbally.
I wear my hair in twists when I feel like holding in my emotions, forming rows
Like cornfields being grown in the golden-dipped sky.

Sometimes I wear my hair in puffs when I'm ecstatic,
Two ponytails that defy gravity,
round like the planets that orbit the sun in the anonymous star-speckled sky.

I wear my hair out, kinks, curls, and all, freely expressing themselves
With no designated destination,
For I wear my metaphoric crown like this when I am in a state of tranquility.

At times I wonder if my hair is too much,
Too loud?
Too expressive?
Too excessive?
Yes,

My hair may be all these things, maybe my hair is eccentric,
It may not fulfill today's rigorous system of beauty,
But it's **mine.**
Mine to express my perplexed feelings to the world,
Mine to tell my story,
Mine to wear.

My hair is a crown that shines like a beacon.
My hair is beautiful,
My hair is a multitude of me.

Category L, Multimedia
MOUNT SINAI MIDDLE SCHOOL
Mrs. Wallace, Grade 8

Grand Champion

There is Time
Paige Sweeney

As the assignments flow in,
As the responsibilities are present,
As the anxiety takes control,
I have no time, I have no time.

The minutes pass while I stare at a molecule
The minutes pass as I sit, exhausted from my day
The minutes pass as I worry about my due dates
The minutes pass as I perfect every answer
The minutes pass as I long for more time.

Yet,
There is time,
There is time for laughter
There is time for joy
There is time to watch the koi circle in the flowing pond.
There is time for perseverance
There is time for rest
There is time to see sunrise and sunset
There is time for care
There is time for growth
There is time for running hand in hand with the ones you love most
There is time for food
There is time for plants
There is time to give creativity a chance
There is time to bake
There is time to read
There is time to walk amongst the trees
There is time to live your life.

I have time, I have time.

OYSTER BAY HIGH SCHOOL
Dr. Faughey, Grade 12

YouTube Link: https://youtu.be/KLNG8dpYmuI

Only Me
Lilly Dejesus

What is me, well many things make up me.
When I see a little sketch, my hand makes up thousands of lines
That form into a shape like a spider...on a web.
As my shape spins like a ballerina finishing her dance, my eyes follow her.
Each cobweb blooms into a misty dream.
As I draw out each stroke on the plump piece of paper,
I click on my broad iPad screen and click on the shiny red button called Youtube.
I hear the voice of Zezre as I work, hearing her opinions calm me down
As I feel like I have a friend around.
As each stroke thickens I start to sketch out the great city of Akihabara
As my mind floats into a foggy state.
The ballerina is at her final dance twirling, leaping and spinning all over the purple desk.
At last, my final piece is finished!

MOUNT SINAI MIDDLE SCHOOL
Mrs. Wallace, Grade 8

The Pursuit
Maiya Staudt

A glass boat set with mirrors sits outside the walls of the Parrish Art Museum.
It is an unassuming and elegant piece,
But if you look inside you'll see the real meaning of it.
Inside of this ship set with mirrors are hundreds of origami boats folded by guests of the museum.
The contents of these boats are unknown to anyone but the writers.
All we know is the prompt:
"What is your idea of a perfect society and how would you get there?"
I think I am similar to this sculpture in many ways;
From the outside I may seem simple and boring,
But on the inside I am full of adventures and creativity,
Similar to how each of the small origami boats are different and unique.
So are my thoughts, interests, and beliefs.
Like this boat, I am large and I contain multitudes.

Category L, Multimedia
MOUNT SINAI MIDDLE SCHOOL
Mrs. Wallace, Grade 8

Category L, Multimedia 123
MOUNT SINAI MIDDLE SCHOOL
Mrs. Wallace, Grade 8

www.ingramcontent.com/pod-product-compliance
Lightning Source LLC
Chambersburg PA
CBHW061737070526
44585CB00024B/2714